From the Author

I hope you enjoy this book as much as I enjoyed preparing it.

John Edmund

May God bless you always — in ALL ways!

EXPONENTIAL
Multiply Your Power To Do Good

EXPONENTIAL
Multiply Your Power To Do Good

JOHN EDMUND HAGGAI

Kobrey Press

Atlanta, Georgia USA

ISBN   978-1-883108-07-6

(cover design by David John Lee)

To my wife Christine

*whose insistence in 1964 that I take the time to visit
the land of my father in the Middle East was used by
God to open my eyes to the strategy required for
world evangelism — a strategy that was new, and yet
as old as the Christian faith.*

CONTENTS

Acknowledgments

I extend my heartfelt thanks to the members of the editorial team who helped to develop this book and get it into print:

David John Lee, an Englishman and Oxford graduate now living in France, has helped me for nearly a quarter of a century. He greatly improves my writings, although I produce the material. I find his perspicacity and lightning-quick analysis somewhat unnerving at times. What a debt I owe him.

Norma Byrd joined my staff more than 34 years ago. She may know my thought processes better than anyone except my wife (frightening thought!). During that time she has served as my literary assistant. In my long ministry — more than 60 years — I have found her second to none in her mastery of grammar and syntax. And she adapts to my style!

Roland Moody worked for years as an executive with Macy's. He advises me regarding distribution. My ministry precludes my involvement in high visibility activities. Furthermore, my time demands preclude my making the circuit for radio, television, and print media interviews — something today's publishers require. Moody arranges for the best possible distribution given my self-imposed limitations.

A fairly recent staff addition, Maya Henderson works with Roland Moody and has given invaluable assistance in proofing this work.

Scott Schreffler retired from his full-time position as H.I. Vice President, Communications in early 2004 after nearly 25 years of service. Scott continues to assist Haggai Institute on a part-time basis as writer, editor, and proofreader. He graciously took time to review *Exponential*.

Last, but by no means least, I salute John Bachman. He has assisted me for 25 years and has spent more time in Haggai Institute travel, meetings, and executive conferences than anyone. He constantly directs my attention to something I have said or written pertinent to the matter at hand. He has mastered the art of detail. When he reports statistics, you can rely upon their accuracy.

PREFACE: EXPONENTIAL

This book contains the essence of my heart and mind on the subject of world evangelism. It is based on some major addresses I made at annual meetings of trustees, supporters, and family members of Haggai Institute for Advanced Leadership.

Each chapter comes at the goal from a different direction. Some points are made in more than one place. I have decided against editing out these overlaps because the points bear repetition and help to make connections between one chapter and another.

The word "exponential" is a crucial concept underlying everything in the pages that follow.

In the United States, there is one senior minister for every 506 people. In other words, the number of senior ministers is now approaching 600,000. That does not include associate pastors, ministers in education, teaching ministers or evangelists.

Apply this percentage to just one country, Bangladesh, with a population of over 130 million. To have the same ratio would require 400,000 in the role of full-time, church-related, Christian witness. That's only one country — a country probably most of my readers did not think to pray for this morning.

Apply the same ratios to the 2.5 billion making up China and India, and the 300 million making up the Arabic-speaking world, and the 200 million in Indonesia. You get the message.

Evangelism capable of reaching every person on the planet must be able to reproduce itself *exponentially*. That is the belief at the heart of Haggai Institute. And it is the argument connecting every chapter in this book.

We have not yet scratched the surface of the opportunity — and responsibility — given by our Lord.

For many years, our Lord's words as recorded in John 14:12 have haunted me. Read them and reflect:

> *Verily, verily, I say unto you, He that believeth on me, the works that I do shall he do also; and greater works than these shall he do; because I go unto my Father.*

I yearn to see that promise fulfilled in my lifetime. He promised it, and His promises are sure.

Earnestly do I pray that the Lord will graciously use this volume to convict and encourage believers — and, yes, even bring some who are in the valley of decision to a commitment of faith in the Lord Jesus Christ.

If you have any questions about any material in this book, do not hesitate to contact me at Haggai Institute, Post Office Box 13, Atlanta, Georgia 30370-2801.

John Edmund

1
SO YOU WANT TO MAKE A DIFFERENCE?

W hat do you plan to do with the rest of your life? How do you want to be remembered? What kind of epitaph do you want the world to chisel on your gravestone?

Most people say, "Well, I want to be remembered as one who made a difference." Well, no Christian would disagree with that, but what kind of a difference do you want to make? Have you planned it in your own mind? Have you worked out the details of how, under God, you're going to make a lasting and a godly impact?

Now here's a shocking thought:

Where will you be in five years?

If you plan no changes in your life, in five years you'll be the same person you are now — or less. Does that fact motivate you? It should. God does not merely wish you to make a difference. He does not merely hope for you to make a difference. He commands it. He tells you to go out there and change things — globally, exponentially.

Don't we most vividly remember the last words of loved ones just before they have been taken from us? I do. Is it not reasonable to think that they considered those words most important? Of course.

Well, what did Jesus talk about just before He left the earth? Did He or did He not speak exclusively about spreading the Gospel to the whole world? And did He not emphasize that command for the entire forty days between His resurrection and His ascension into Heaven?

Examine the language that Jesus uses. What are we to do?

- Make disciples.
- Preach the Gospel.
- Preach repentance and remission of sins.
- Witness.

But that's only half of it. That's the *function*. Then there's the *area of function*. And when you discount the area, you have disobeyed the command. You cannot segment God's commands.

Half obedience is disobedience.

Jesus says, "Go." To all nations — really the word is *ethne* — all ethnic groups. From *Jerusalem to the uttermost part of the earth*. For too many Christians, that translates as "within a two-mile radius of our church."

God bless those whose vision stretches beyond the horizon.

My mother carried on a tract ministry in the Brockton, Massachusetts, bus depot. Every week she replenished the supply on the tract rack that she had installed. Many came to know the Lord. Some of them wrote her. But Mother knew that while it was important, it did not equate with obedience to the Great Commission, because it did not go from Jerusalem unto the uttermost parts of the earth.

So every month she and Dad reproduced a missionary letter. With their slim income, they paid for the postage and mailed it out to people across the nation, asking them to pray for the missionaries and hoping that they would give.

They themselves always devoted a certain amount of their time and energy and money to the uttermost parts of the earth. They understood there is no such thing as obedience to half a command.

You want to make a difference? I'll be frank with you. Your life will never attain optimum significance apart from total obedience to the Lord's command to take the Gospel to the entire world.

That's categorical.

Total obedience — or disobedience

I'm just passing on to you what I've been living for the last eighty years. There's far too much clever talk in the Western church. Far too many complicated excuses for not doing what God has patently made a priority.

Obeying the Great Commission — and I mean obeying it in the terms in which it was given, not in some emasculated version we happen to find convenient — is the key to doing good in the twenty-first century.

Without it, you will accomplish nothing of lasting significance. With it, you will light a fire for God. A fire for change that can spread, with no further input from you, at an *exponential* rate.

In my view, that's something worth being remembered for.

2
YOU EITHER SEE IT
OR YOU DON'T

He was only 42 years old. The late Cecil Day asked me to join him for lunch in his private dining room. For more than three hours he poured out his heart.

I was able to read his spiritual EKG; and every spike, both up and down, revealed his passion for evangelism.

Every 20 minutes or so, his executive assistant, Mrs. Jo Dollar, came to the dining room. He dismissed her each time with a request for her to cancel his engagement at that given time.

A few days later, his attorney said, "Dr. Haggai, I understand you and Cecil had a conference that lasted more than three hours. He never meets with anyone for more than ten minutes." Only then did I grasp the importance Cecil had attached to the autobiographical insights he gave me. They all fit neatly into a package you could label "World Evangelism Today."

Political correctness never trimmed his passion. Elitist peer pressure never diffused his laser-like focus. Socially popular trivia never diluted his determination. His life reflected the spirit of the apostle who announced, *"None of these things move me."*

Cecil's passion for evangelism — beginning at home in Georgia, moving to New England, and then to the ends of the earth — embraced the globe. His heart was 25,000 miles in circumference. His arms embraced every color, every creed, every tongue, every echelon of society, every rank of culture, every stratum of intellectuality.

His priority focused on global evangelism. Single-handedly and on borrowed money, he bought the center on Ridout Road in the upscale section of Singapore and gave it to Haggai Institute.

On the other side of the Pacific, shipping tycoon and ordained clergyman Canon Yip Tung Shan and his attorney son-in-law (later Justice of the Supreme Court) Lai Kew Chai opened doors to this ministry that now penetrates 178 nations. (Data on the numbers trained by Haggai Institute is revised upwards every month. This figure was correct at the time of writing.)

These two stellar leaders, youthful Cecil Burke Day and senior Canon Yip, were committed to evangelism.

Cecil Day died at age 44. I shall never forget how his young widow Deen riveted the crowd at the annual meeting in 1979 with her address that ended with the words: "I cannot fill his shoes, but I can step in his tracks."

God raised up in those early days other donors who shared the young tycoon's passion: James I. "Mac" McCormick, Guy Rutland, Arnold Browning, Ernest and Ella Watson, W. A. and Mildred Haggai, Bud Lindsey, Hank McCamish, to mention a few.

Our trustees worldwide are committed to evangelism. Our faculty members are committed to evangelism. Our alumni are committed to evangelism.

We believe Jesus Christ is the only answer to every problem confronting mankind today. The Bible makes this clear. History underscores it. Personal experience corroborates it.

World evangelism changed the world

Consider how God has blessed the world through evangelism.

Who did more for education than Russell Conwell? His concern originated with his commitment to Jesus Christ. His work in education — the establishment of Temple University — has impacted every continent for good.

Who did more for the working man than England's Lord Shaftesbury? His concern originated with his commitment to Christ.

Who did more for youth, through his personal ministry and through the YMCA, than D.L. Moody? His great work originated with his commitment to Christ.

Who did more for the poor than General William Booth and his Salvation Army? His concern originated with his commitment to Christ.

Who did more for social reform than John Wesley? His effectiveness originated with his Aldersgate experience when he committed his life to the Lord Jesus Christ at the age of 38, after he had taught at Oxford and served as a missionary to the colony of Georgia.

The impact of this preaching of the message of evangelism was to be felt all over the world. John Howard instituted prison reforms in Europe in the 1770s. J. Hudson Taylor founded the China Inland Mission in 1865. John Barnardo began his mission work in London in 1867, which resulted in the rescuing and reclaiming of 70,000 waifs. In the United States, Princeton University, the University of Pennsylvania, and many other universities stand as tributes to the preaching of the message of evangelism by William Tennent and George Whitefield.

In his day, who did more for the black community than William Wilberforce, the man who in 1807 single-handedly rammed through the British Parliament a bill bringing an end to slave trading? His concern began with his commitment to Christ in a John Wesley revival meeting.

Who did more to change the social, moral, and political complexion of Southeast Asia than Dr. John Sung? His unparalleled influence for good began with his commitment to Christ.

Who has so influenced the great nation of Korea — with its unprecedented spiritual revival, its proliferation of orphanages, universities, hospitals, and beneficent penetration in all areas of society — as Dr. Han Kyung Chik? His great work began with his commitment to Jesus Christ.

What do we need to understand about the message of evangelism?

The message meets the real need

In Romans 1:16, Paul said, *"I am not ashamed of the Gospel."* Literally, that translates as, "I am not ashamed of evangelism."

In verse 17, Paul defines this message — the message of evangelism, the Gospel message — as *"the revelation of the righteousness of God."*

The righteousness of God is that attribute of His nature that requires Him to demand righteousness in man. God is righteous and, therefore, He can neither condone nor commune with sin. In the words of the prophet Habakkuk, He is *"of purer eyes than to behold evil, and canst not look on iniquity"* (Habakkuk 1:13).

Man sinned. Sin is rebellion against God whether active or passive. In sinning, he severed his relationship with God. Man's only access to God was by meeting the demands of Divine righteousness. This he could not do.

You cannot do it. I cannot do it. But then, in stepped the Lord Jesus Christ:

> *For He* [God] *made Him who knew no sin to be sin for us, that we might become the righteousness of God in Him* (2 Corinthians 5:21).

In Christ, man meets the demands of Divine righteousness. In Christ, he has access to God.

Only in Christ does man have union with God. In Christ, the total resources of God are made available.

Any "Gospel" — any purported message of evangelism — that does not reveal Christ as God's total deliverance for man's total depravity is a false Gospel and unworthy of half a hallelujah.

The unbelievers of this world have vied with each other in their efforts to reveal Jesus.

Pilate called Him "the man without fault."

Diderot called Him "the unsurpassed."

Napoleon called Him "the emperor of love."

David Strauss called Him "the highest model of religion."

Leckey called Him "the highest pattern of virtue."

Renan called Him "the greatest among the sons of men."

Theodore Parker called Him "the youth with God in his heart."

Some of our contemporaries have referred to Him as simply "the man upstairs"!

None of these adequately explains Christ. Only the Gospel — the message of evangelism — reveals Christ as the God-man, the One in whom dwells *"all the fullness of the Godhead bodily."*

This message of evangelism, which reveals the totality of God's revelation to man in Christ, is our only hope.

In fifty or a hundred years, if God spares the human race, some ethereal-minded, Bible-scorning, bleeding hearts may endeavor to take over this ministry. That has been the history of so many Christ-honoring institutions. I want it on the record that Haggai Institute was founded and organized by men and women — clergy and laity — who believed in Jesus Christ. They believed that He, preexistent throughout all eternity — before His birth to the Virgin Mary — suffered and died for the sins of all humankind. They believed that He rose again by the power of God, ascended to Heaven, and will return to earth a second time, in glory.

The message of evangelism meets man in the totality of his real needs. *"It is the power of God unto salvation to everyone that believeth"* (Romans 1:16).

Sin is rampant. Sensualism turns the hands of our contemporary timepiece to "sex o'clock" as nymphomania becomes the chief moral and psychological disorder of the day. Secularism, with a penknife of a Jehoiakim, cuts out all Bible passages bespeaking the supernatural. Skepticism intoxicates thousands of our college youth with the sparkling wine of pseudo-intellectualism. Multitudes of church members have joined in the festivities around the golden calf of worldliness.

At this hour, sinners sleep in the darkness while saints sleep in the light. With these Scripturally ignorant, spiritually perverted multitudes, Satan has succeeded in substituting humanism in philosophy and hedonism in daily living for a vital relationship with Jesus Christ.

And, especially among Westerners, spurious celebrity-itis has replaced spiritual commitment. Obsessions for recognition, for power, for honor, and the mindless expenditures of money to gratify carnal drug-like desires have replaced vital godliness.

The message of evangelism is the only answer to man in his real needs.

The message is the power of God

The message of evangelism is the power of God. The word in the original Greek text, *dunamis*, is the root from which we get the English words dynamic and dynamite. This divine dynamite smashes to bits the citadel of sin that Satan has established in the human heart.

Consider the power of God. We, with our intercontinental ballistic missiles and twenty-first century technology, think we are the quintessence of power.   But in reality we are mere pygmies, occupying one of God's smaller planets.

Divine power! By it, God, who set a tabernacle in the heavens for the sun, hangs the earth upon nothing. By it, God stretches forth the dark canopy of night and pins it back with clusters of fixed stars. The nearest star to earth, Alpha Centauri, is so far away that if we were to get on a train and travel there at sixty miles an hour by day and by night, we would not arrive for forty-eight million years!

Divine power! By it, a single pound of ordinary matter contains enough energy to have driven all the ships of the pre-World War II U.S. Navy from New York to Liverpool, England, and halfway back again.

God tells us through the Psalmist:

By the word of the Lord were the heavens made and all the host of them by the breath of His mouth (Psalm 33:6).

In another place we read, *"He spake and it was done"* (verse 9).

Yet the power whereby God created the world and the stellar universe could not save man from his sin and deliver him from his bondage. God could not speak our salvation. Our salvation taxed the resources of God. It demanded the death of God in Christ. Don't ever forget that the man on the middle cross was God.

Until the dynamite of God, working through the revelation of Christ, blows the wiring to bits, the sinner is merely the devil's robot. He does that which Satan dictates. Paul says he walks *"according to the prince of the power of the air, the spirit that now worketh in* [literally, energizes] *the children of disobedience"* (Ephesians 2:2).

Only the Divine Dynamite of God can deliver a man from the power of the world, the flesh, and the devil. Only the Divine Dynamite of God can give victory over a heart that *"is deceitful above all things, and desperately wicked"*(Jeremiah 17:9).

The revelation of Christ received by faith makes men new creatures. Old things pass away. All things become new.

The message of evangelism was powerful enough to take the strategy chief of the Mau-Maus in Africa — a man who had to prove his loyalty to the Mau-Maus by agreeing to stomp to death his mother and father on command — and change him into an apostle of love. I thank God that he is a Haggai Institute alumnus and serves the Lord faithfully on his great continent.

The message of evangelism was powerful enough to take an Indonesian Communist, who had slain many innocent people and served years in prison, and convert him to a child of light and love. He now shares the message of our redemptive Christ with his people in the world's fourth largest nation.

In 1944, I was driving back to Chicago from a youth rally in Hobart, Indiana. Four cars piled up because of a nearly fatal error by the driver of the first car. I was in the fourth car — the last in line.

The police came to the accident location, measured the skid marks, and recorded all the observable data. They turned to me first and said, "You were within the purview of the law. You may go home."

I looked at the wreck that had been my car, and asked, "How?"

They said, "If you hurry, you can catch the last interurban train to Chicago before daybreak."

I and my five passengers pooled our limited resources and barely eked out enough money for the train tickets to Chicago. In fact, we were so broke that we had to walk the three miles from Chicago's Union Station to the dormitory. We couldn't afford streetcar fare.

Two weeks later, I was the unwitting host of an unwelcome guest who introduced himself as an officer of the court.

He said, "I'm serving you these papers."

I said, "Why?"

"You were involved in an accident outside of Hobart, Indiana."

I said, "Wait a minute. I was within the purview of the law. The police exonerated me."

He said, "That may be, but these other drivers are suing you. It's a civil suit. They are all from Indiana."

For several days, in a dejected frame of mind, I kept walking all over my lower lip. Then, one day, my good friend Dick Stanley came to me and said, "John, you look like you are in trouble." I said, "If you don't think I'm in trouble, put a cork on top of my head, and see how long it stays there." I explained my situation.

He said, "You need to see Weinstein."

Now I had done my research, and I knew that Weinstein was the top-rated and most expensive accident lawyer in Chicago. I also knew I couldn't afford the striping on the wallpaper in just one room of his office suite. Yet Dick Stanley glibly said, "See Weinstein."

I said, "Dick, a cow just flew over the moon. I can't afford Weinstein."

"Ah," he said, "John, Arrow Engineering Service that I own retains him. We pay him a lot of money every year."

Then Dick Stanley whipped out a business card, scribbled a note over his illegible signature, and said, "Give him this card. He'll see you."

I bounded up to my one-room, third-floor apartment to dress for the visit to the famous attorney. Back in those days, I had a suit for every day in the week. It was salt-and-pepper tweed. We didn't send our suits to the cleaners; we put them in the refrigerator. I put on my suit. I put on my red tie and my brown Thom McAn shoes.

I had ten cents. The streetcar cost seven cents. I thought it would be preferable not to be perspiring when I visited him. I therefore decided to take the streetcar to Chicago's famed loop and walk back.

I entered the posh office building overwhelmed by its grandeur. In a moment, I was catapulted in a pre-jet-age, supersonic elevator to floor eighteen. It was the first time I had ever seen wall-to-wall carpeting on the corridors of an office building.

I made my way to Weinstein's office, opened the door. A lady, poor dear, didn't have enough money to buy total glasses; she just had half of them! Perched behind an antique typewriter, she looked up at me, ignored me, and went back to work. She could tell by the cut of my clothes — that little old sack suit hiked at the back and dipped at the points — that I was in the wrong pew.

Well, the Lord has given me one trait — I don't give up easily. I stuck Dick Stanley's card under her two eyeballs. In less time than it takes to say, "Weinstein," I was ushered into the "sanctum sanctorum" of the brainiest Jewish lawyer I've ever met in my life. And when you get a Syrian to pay a tribute like that to a Jew, that guy's a genius!

He said, "Tell me your problem."

I told him.

He said, "You have no problem."

I looked at him wide-eyed and said, "Well, I've been laboring under a horrible delusion these last two weeks."

Weinstein replied, "No, no, here's the answer...."
He outlined the steps — one, two, three, four.

It was really no problem.

Now, I had three cents in my pocket after the carfare. Do you think I opened my hand, exposing my three pennies, and said, "How much do I owe you, Mr. Weinstein?" He would have thrown me out of the window.

Why did Weinstein see me? Because he liked the heroic proportions of my Phoenician profile? No — magnificent as it is! Was it because he was trying to improve Arab/Jewish relations? No. Because he thought I was a promising young man? No.

He saw me through the merits of, and on the basis of, the fee payment by Dick Stanley and the Arrow Engineering Service. And every resource he had that was available to Dick Stanley was available to me. Dick Stanley, by love, related himself to me. But I had to come to Weinstein and present my credentials. I had to willingly admit my need. On Stanley's account, Weinstein accepted me.

I had a need. Weinstein had the answer for the need. I didn't have the fee. Dick Stanley had paid the fee. I came in the name and through the fee payment of Dick Stanley, and the entire resources of the brilliant Weinstein were available to me. My problem — my need — was met.

Now I have a spiritual need — the need for salvation. But salvation is of the Lord. And I cannot get to Him, because I am a sinner. Remember, sin is separation. Sin has separated me from God. God said through the prophet Isaiah, *"But your iniquities have separated you from your God; and your sins have hidden His face from you, so that he will not hear"* (Isaiah 59:2).

In our sins we are isolated from God, deprived of all His blessings. But here's good news — the message of evangelism:

> *When He* [Jesus] *saw that we were partakers of flesh and blood, He Himself also took part of the same that through death* [remember, death means separation] *He might destroy him that had the power of death, that is, the devil* (Hebrews 2:14).

I am separated from God by sin. Unless I can pay the fee for my spiritual debt, I shall die. That means, I shall forever be separated from God. But I can't pay the fee. The fee payment is death. *"The soul that sinneth, it shall die"* (Ezekiel 18:20).

You can't pay the fee for me. You're a sinner, and one bankrupt can't pay the bills of another bankrupt. Jesus was without sin. He could — and did — pay the fee. Not in dollars and cents — not with corruptible silver and gold, as the apostle Peter reminds us — but with His own incorruptible blood.

Just as my legal need was met by Weinstein through Dick Stanley, who paid the fee, so my spiritual, my eternal, need is met through Jesus who paid the fee — who "paid it all."

The message works

Salvation is a comprehensive term embracing all of God's blessings to man in Christ. Salvation is the inclusion of all good for every part of the composite nature of man.

The message of evangelism not only reveals this fact to man but also gives man the ability to respond to it by faith.

The Grecian says, "Man, know thyself."

The Roman says, "Man, rule thyself."

The Chinese says, "Man, improve thyself."

The Buddhist says, "Man, annihilate thyself."

The Brahman says, "Man, submerge thyself in the universal sum of all."

The modern internationalist says, "Man, learn the art and practice the principles of peaceful coexistence."

But Christ says, *"Without me, you can do nothing."*

The Gospel of Jesus Christ produces morals that can never be realized apart from it. The Gospel of Jesus Christ produces ethical purity that can never be realized without it. The Gospel of Jesus Christ produces a social concern in the hearts of individuals — a concern that legislation and education combined can never produce.

It was John Morley, the noted British author, who gave this significant testimony. "We all have been upon the wrong track." He complained further, "And the result is that the whole of us have less to show for our work than one man, Booth of the Salvation Army.

"Herbert Spencer, Matthew Arnold, Frederick Harrison, and the rest of us, who have spent our lives in endeavoring to dispel superstition and to bring on a new era, must admit that Booth has had more direct effect upon this generation than all of us put together. General Booth made personal regeneration basic, and social reform followed. His work was wholly Christian and Biblical — the proclamation of the message of evangelism."

On the island of Bali lives a Haggai Institute alumnus who has brought a village from the Stone Age into the twenty-first century. He has shown the people how to make bricks, fish farm, convert pig manure into LP gas, and utilize solar energy.

Each night he taught this message of evangelism to the people who would sit under his vocational instruction the next day. In fact, if they didn't come to the Christian service at night, they missed out on the vocational input the following day.

In that group were two men, former Communists, who beheaded the four brothers of our alumnus. They did not know he was aware of their identity — so great was the love of Christ communicated through this remarkable man. You talk about the social and economic betterment of humankind? Surpass that, if you can.

In all of these instances — and thousands more that I could give you — personal regeneration has been the base. The message of evangelism has been the foundation.

> *Even the righteousness of God which is by faith of Jesus Christ unto all and upon all them that believe: for there is no difference* (Romans 3:22).

The Gospel of Jesus Christ is never out of date and never in the wrong place. That's why we sing:

To the ends of the earth is our aim
To bring to the lost Jesus' name.
With the Gospel story,
We will march on to glory.
To the ends of the earth is our aim.

Paul says *"there is neither Greek nor Jew* [no racial barrier], *circumcision nor uncircumcision* [no ceremonial barrier], *Barbarian, Scythian* [no national barrier], *bond nor free* [no social barrier], *but Christ is all and in all"* (Colossians 3:11).

So why be ashamed of evangelism?

Paul said, *"I am not ashamed."*
Why should any man who calls himself a Christian be ashamed of this glorious message by which he was released and redeemed? Why should he be ashamed to share with man the only answer to his real needs? Why should he be ashamed of Jesus Christ our Lord, who is the Animator of all true progress, the Transformer of the world's ills?
Without shame, without embarrassment, let us address ourselves to this glorious opportunity. By our lips and by our lives let's show the people that we, too, are *"not ashamed."* We are proud of this message of evangelism — God's authoritative word to modern man.

We shall fight, and we shall win. But the weapons of our warfare are not carnal. There is no secret weapon, no hush-hush H-bomb, no sophisticated thermonuclear devices. Our weapons we can announce to the whole world. No one can destroy them. They are immune to terror. They are the weapons of love and prayer. They require the backing of no numerical balance of power.

And we shall not be ashamed!

It is conceivable that some — perhaps many — shall seal their testimony with the color of their blood. But, even in dying, we shall evangelize — declaring the fact that a loving God has made the only adequate provision for humankind.

He sent His Son, the Lord Jesus Christ, as His bread for man's hunger, His water for man's thirst, His light for man's darkness, His peace for man's perplexity, His fullness for man's emptiness, His salvation for man's sin. That's good news. That's evangelism. That's what we believe. That's why we are here. That's the purpose for which Haggai Institute exists.

And we shall not be ashamed!

God helping us, we shall evangelize in the cities. We shall evangelize in the villages. We shall evangelize in the jungles. We shall evangelize in the pulpit, in the press, in the electronic media, on the stage. We shall evangelize in season and out of season, in freedom and in jail, in health and in sickness, in our labor and in our leisure. We shall evangelize in the corridors of academia, in the halls of government, in the wards of our hospitals, in the offices of commerce.

And we shall not be ashamed!

Enemies of the cross thought they had exterminated the message when they martyred Paul the apostle. But Edward Gibbon, the historian who tells us about the decline and fall of Rome, identifies the preaching of Paul as one of the contributing factors to the dissolution of that corrupt body politic.

In his own strength, Saul, the terrible, the murderer, was unable to implement his desires to commit genocide against the people of God. But, once committed to the Lord Jesus Christ, he changed the world with the weapons of love and prayer and witness.

In my mind's eye, I see the apostle Paul yanked from the Mamertine dungeon and led to the place of his execution beside a pool west of Rome. I hear the imps of Tophet, the demons of Hell, whispering in his ear, "Aren't you ashamed, Paul? You could have been head of the philosophy department at the Hebrew University. Instead you have chosen to be a fanatical missionary evangelist."

I see the little apostle, shriveled to four-feet-eleven, according to tradition. His brow is wrinkled, and he, with weak eyes, squints under the unsullied purity of the noonday sun. But he responds, "Not ashamed."

"What about when you were imperiled for your life in Damascus?"

"Not ashamed."

"What about when you were accursed at Corinth?"

"Not ashamed."

"What about when you were mocked at Athens?"

"Not ashamed."

"What about when you were cursed at Berea?"

"Not ashamed."

"What about when you were stoned and left for dead at Lystra?"

"Not ashamed."

"What about when you were shipwrecked on your way to Rome?"

"Not ashamed."

"What about your two years being chained like a caged animal to a praetorian guard?"

"Not ashamed."

"What about your two years in this miserable dungeon, living with vermin and rats and on starvation rations?"

"Not ashamed."

"What about when they wanted to dedicate a street in your honor, and instead you trekked across the dusty roadways of the remotest lands?"

"Not ashamed."

"What about when you were offered a testimonial dinner, and you decided instead, to go to Philippi where they threw you in jail?"

"Not ashamed."

"What about your invitation to meet with the political leaders, and instead you kept babbling about wanting to go to Illyricum where no one had heard of Christ?"

"Not ashamed."

"What about when they wanted to honor you at a national day celebration, and instead you chose yet another missionary trip where you were mauled by the beasts, mistreated by felons, and mocked by the religious leaders?"

"Not ashamed."

"You really are a fanatic, Paul."

"Not ashamed."

And I see the dauntless warrior, as he lifts the trumpet of no uncertain sound to his lips and blasts off:

> *For the which cause I suffer these things. Nevertheless, I'm not ashamed, for I know whom I have believed and am persuaded that He is able to be my "safety deposit vault"* [that's the better translation] *against that day. I have fought a good fight, I have finished my course, I have kept the faith: Henceforth, there is a crown of righteousness reserved for me, which I shall happily cast at my Savior's feet* (2 Timothy 1:12, 4:7-8).

Paul was one of those rare individuals who fulfilled his commitment after the environment in which he made it had dissipated. He understood the power of the permanent.

He was not addicted to the "Project of the Month" mentality. He recognized that we are all going to stand before the Bema, the Judgment Seat of Christ, and give an answer for every idle word, for every idle deed — not just bad words and not just bad deeds — for every dollar misspent, for every hour squandered, for every influence not exploited for the glory of Christ — and for every opportunity not seized.

He was not ashamed of evangelism.

Oh, the frustration I feel in my inability to express through my lips the emotions that break the backs of words. I understand well the words that Shakespeare put into the mouth of Mark Anthony after Brutus had killed Caesar. Mark Anthony said,

> *I am no orator, as Brutus is;*
> . . . .
> *For I have neither wit, nor words, nor worth,*
> *Action, nor utterance, nor power of speech,*
> *To stir men's blood. I only speak right on;*
> *I tell you that which you yourselves do know;*
> *Show you sweet Caesar's wounds,*
> *poor poor dumb mouths,*
> *And bid them speak for me: but were I Brutus,*
> *And Brutus Anthony, there were an Anthony*
> *Would ruffle up your spirits, and put a tongue*
> *In every wound of Caesar, that should move*
> *The stones of Rome to rise and mutiny.*

So say I, dear friends. I am no orator, but let every wound of Jesus' bleeding body be a mouth, and we should hear in jubilant chorus: *I am thy salvation. I have blotted out like a cloud thy sins and like a thick cloud thine iniquities. As My Father hath sent Me, so send I you.* (See Psalm 35:3; Isaiah 44:21-23; John 20:21.)

May it be the passion in our hearts which melts the lead in our feet and the ice on our tongues, and drives us to full obedience, recognizing this truth:

"Only one life, 'twill soon be past.
Only what's done for Christ will last."

It's that passion that explodes into the confession:
I AM NOT ASHAMED!

3
IMPOSSIBLE
IS THE WHOLE POINT

Haggai Institute was conceived through faith. It was launched through faith. It was funded through faith. It grew through faith. It continues to move to the outer limits of Christ's precisely defined commission — through faith.

What kind of faith do I mean? Simple: the kind of faith that, by seeing the invisible, accomplishes the impossible.

The kind of faith that has trained over 65,500 world leaders — and growing at 8 percent a year— who have, in turn, trained millions of national leaders for evangelism

The kind of faith that has brought 178 nations a fresh and powerful encounter with the Gospel.

The kind of faith that has raised millions of dollars for a ministry based ten thousand miles away, while maintaining — with some difficulty — a near-zero profile at home.

The kind of faith that has survived the martyrdom of five alumni (that we know of).

The kind of faith that by prayer, love, commitment, and sacrifice has reached the leading edge and determined not only to live there but, if necessary, to die there.

The kind of faith *"without which,"* as the Word tells us, *"it is impossible to please God"* (1 John 5:4b;

2 Corinthians 5:7; Hebrews 11:6).

John writes in his first epistle: *"This is the victory that has overcome the world, even our faith"* (1 John 5:4). Love dreams of victory. Hope clings to victory. Vision plans for victory. But faith *is* the victory.

In the late 1960s, a group of women and men agreed with me on certain self-evident truths. They took the Great Commission seriously. Many glibly recite it, but these folks acted on it. Faith is acting on the thing you say you believe as though it were so.

They obeyed the command of Jesus: *"Make disciples of all nations"* (Matthew 28:19). The word "nations" comes from the Greek word *ethne*, which means "peoples" or "ethnic groups."

At that time, more than 2.2 billion knew nothing about the Lord Jesus. Do you know how many today have never heard about the Lord Jesus? In the nations of India and China alone, they outnumber the population of the entire Western hemisphere by a factor of three. Eighty-five percent (85%) of the world's unevangelized are off-limits to Western missionaries.

Make disciples of all nations? Is it reasonable to conclude that Jesus mocks us with an impossibility? Can a thoughtful person believe that the Great Commissioner commissions us to failure?

Haggai Institute's founding trustees and donors believed, really believed, the Great Commission. How else can you explain their undertaking such an unprecedented global program? Tackling such a task bordered on insanity, humanly speaking. They took responsibility for a concept that was untried, untested, and ridiculed by some of God's choicest servants — including Western missiologists, mission-minded pastors, and the former head of the National Association of Evangelicals (who was also a good friend).

Haggai Institute's early supporters did not accommodate their faith to their comfort zones. They acted on the vision. Remember: faith is acting upon the thing you say you believe as though it were true. They risked the required innovation for a totally new pattern of world evangelism. They didn't pontificate with sterile words like, "God can give victory." It doesn't take a Ph.D. to figure that one out; that takes no faith. They declared, "God will give victory." And He did, and He does. That's the result of God's work through faith.

Yesterday

God gave Elijah a vision of rain to end the drought. Did Elijah do nothing? No. Faith impelled him to implement the vision. He demonstrated his faith by works.

See the prophet run to the mountaintop. Catch a glimpse of him putting his head between his knees and pouring out his "effectual, fervent prayer." How long did he pray? He continued in fervent prayer while his servant, dispatched by the prophet seven times, went out to monitor the sky. After the seventh trip, the servant said, *"I saw a cloud the size of a man's hand"* (1 Kings 18:44). Elijah knew the prayer had been answered — the vision fulfilled, the faith rewarded. Only then did he cease his praying for rain.

God's promise of a blessing does not relieve one of praying fervently for the blessing promised. Read 1 Kings 18, especially verses 42b-45.

God gave Noah a vision of the earth purified by a catastrophic flood. Noah believed God. He started work on an ark. He kept at it for 120 years. Neither fatigue nor criticism stopped him. The rains came; the floods rose; the ark brought mankind to a new beginning.

You could go through most of Hebrews 11 to illustrate the point, but I am going to bring you up to date.

It wearies me to hear people predict revival when its preconditions — faith and action — are so conspicuously absent. They are like men who shout "The train's arriving!" at a station with no tracks. Contrast that with Dr. Han of Korea.

More than half a century ago, God gave our first senior faculty member, Dr. Han Kyung Chik, a vision of revival in Korea. Dr. Han acted on the vision in faith. Three times the Communists dispossessed him. More than once he was tortured for his beliefs. He fled to South Korea, and in 1946 established a church with just 27 North Korean refugees. Then, in 1950, came the Communist onslaught from the north. They pushed the South Koreans south — all the way to Pusan, nearly into the sea.

Dr. Han led dawn prayer meetings. Thousands met for prayer from five to six o'clock every morning.

In each city where the refugees stopped, Dr. Han encouraged them to build a church.

In Taegu. In Taejon. In Pusan.

Today, Dr. Han's Young Nak Presbyterian Church in Seoul, numbering more than 60,000 members, with a budget in excess of $70,000,000, touches the whole world. Under his pastoral leadership,Young Nak Church established more than 500 daughter churches, including the Young Nak Church in Downey, California, which in 20 years became the third largest church in California.

When Southern Baptists moved into Korea in 1951, it was Presbyterian Dr. Han who provided them building space until they could acquire their own.

Dr. David Yonggi Cho, founding pastor of the world's largest congregation — more than 850,000 members and a budget in excess of a half billion dollars — cites Dr. Han as a major source of inspiration. Substantially through Dr. Han's influence, Korea's Christian population was doubling every ten years at least to the mid-1990s.

God gave Dr. Han the vision that defined Korea's future. Faith validated by works brought the vision to fulfillment.

Today

God gave us the vision — a vision that saw the Gospel reaching every person in his own language and culture — and God used faith to make the vision real.

Today more than 65,500 nationals working in 178 nations have been trained in Haggai Institute programs. We estimate that they have transferred their training to at least two million of their fellow nationals — though the real figure is probably much higher.

Today, we see how God rewarded the faith of Cecil B. Day, who gave money he didn't have — more than $1.7 million in today's dollars — for the Day Center in Singapore.

Cecil built about 40,000 motel rooms in four years. He built more rooms faster than have ever been built in that same time frame.

Millions of dollars of construction were underway in the 1970s when the oil embargo hit. He was paying 15 percent interest on construction loans which he expected to convert to 9 percent interest on conventional loans when the rooms were completed.

The lack of liquidity torpedoed that possibility. Consequently, he was saddled with millions of dollars of debt.

He visited three bankers every day, five days a week, for 21 months. He told them that he could not pay them. He told them he would understand if they decided to foreclose; but he convinced them that if they went along with him, they would get every penny — which they did.

In the nadir of that problem, H.I. was hoping to buy a prime property in Singapore. It was going to cost about $780,000 in 1977. Cecil had $530,000 to make a payment to a banker in Dallas. He said, "I'll trust God to touch the heart of the banker so he'll roll over the loan."

He did and the banker responded favorably.

Cecil took that $530,000 and arranged for another $250,000, 8 percent loan for eighteen months.

That enabled us to buy the facility in Singapore, which we named the Day Center (over his protest).

He believed that God had given him assurance that the money would become available. That assurance did not end his activity. In fact, he, like Elijah, made fervent prayer that God would speak to the banker and make available the facility.

God rewarded the faith of Guy Rutland, who gave each month more than $20,000 in today's dollars, plus another $300,000 (in today's dollars) each December to underwrite sponsorships. By the way, he and Marie lived as modestly as my wife Christine and I live — though they didn't have to.

God rewarded the faith of Waddy and Mildred Haggai, who gave so generously — above their 20 percent to their church — that at Waddy's death there was a surplus over the five-year carry-forward allowed for income tax purposes.

God rewarded the faith of Phil Gordon, who one year sacrificed time and money to make eleven trips to Atlanta from Lansing, Michigan. Why? To save the financial situation — to keep a half-closed door from being slammed shut completely.

Peter Gill's testimony, delivered to a packed-out Hope Chapel on Maui, still reverberates through the chambers of my mind and heart. This Pakistani riveted the large congregation with his story.

His father received Haggai Institute training in Singapore in 1971. He said he previously had no goals and was rather narrow-minded in his view. He returned from Singapore on fire with a passion to reach souls.

He started reaching Muslims through literature and open-air meetings. He organized a march for Jesus after getting permission from authorities to use a PA system. He also got permission from the authorities to celebrate Christmas, Easter, and Independence Day for Pakistan with a Christian service.

Peter, the only Christian in his university, majored in Islamic studies and political science. He studied Islam deliberately, so he could be a more effective evangelist. It gave him opportunities to talk about Christ with his teachers and fellow students — prominent leaders and future leaders. And he knew how to do it, because his father had passed on the training.

One day, as Peter was organizing a mass distribution of literature in Karachi, near the tomb of Mohammed Ali Jinnah, the founder of Pakistan, a Muslim Imam confronted him. The Imam threatened to have him killed. Peter didn't take it too seriously. The people were reading the literature, "Good News for Karachi." They were hungry for the Word of God. So Peter just moved on to another part of the city. Soon afterwards, he was attacked.

The Imam had sent spies after him. These men

dragged him back to the mosque. They burned his books. They beat him, cutting his forehead with a wooden rod. They threatened to kill him if he didn't stop evangelizing. Peter prayed. First, he said, "Lord, I'm willing to die for you if you want me to." And second, he said, "Lord, raise someone up, if I die, to take the Gospel to the Muslims in my place."

Then he recalled the prayer of Stephen being stoned by the persecutors with Saul of Tarsus standing close by. It was the same prayer of Jesus on the Cross, *"Father, forgive them, they don't know what they're doing"* (Luke 23:34; Acts 7:60).

At that moment the group leader — a tall, strong man returned. He broke up the lynch mob, and took Peter to a nearby hospital where they put four stitches in his forehead. This man paid for the medication and the treatment. He personally washed Peter's face. Then he asked where Peter lived and took him home. He refused compensation for the medical fees. He told Peter, "I am very embarrassed by what happened — please forgive me."

Peter answered, "I've already prayed for you and forgiven you." Then the man wanted to know why Peter had smiled when he was beaten.

Peter quoted Matthew 5:11, *"Blessed are you when they revile and persecute you, and say all kinds of evil against you falsely for my sake. Rejoice and be exceedingly glad . . . ."* He asked if the man wanted to know more, and when he said, "Yes," he presented the Gospel to him. After prayer together, the young man had a tear in his eye. Peter gave him a Bible, and he promised to read it.

Out of that incident a new ministry arose. Peter started a Bible study group for "seekers." In that Muslim nation, he had eight regular participants and about 1,000 doing correspondence studies. Some of them followed the Lord in baptism. Most surprising, every one of the five men who attacked Peter came to Christ.

Powerful! It's a snapshot of the kinds of things Haggai Institute alumni are doing across the globe. But it also illustrates a vital truth.

For years I've talked about the never-changing Gospel in the ever-changing world.

On the basis of that philosophy, Haggai Institute refuses to get locked into a mold. Only the message remains changeless; the method moves with the times. The subject matter in one core course has changed radically since our first seminar in 1969. Why? Because the world has changed.

When I first visited Jakarta, Indonesia, in 1967, I could get to anyone in either their residence or office. Today, limited-access, high-rise apartments, gated communities with sealed-off residences, and unlisted phones transform methods of contact. That requires a massive change in the way one engages in personal evangelism.

But it shouldn't trick us into thinking that evangelism is something you do through a TV set.

Many myths today rob Christians of God's maximum blessings. One of the most insidious is the high-tech myth, the myth that you can effectively win the world for Christ by using only satellite-communicated television. I will illustrate.

In 1972, I met with some espionage agents — both Western and Communist — in the Hilton Hotel outside Addis Ababa. A Communist agent said, "You may have the best satellite surveillance in the world. You can count the dimples on a golf ball rolling toward the green. You can quantify the speed and identify the direction. So what? While you're doing that, I'm swimming in the Gulf with the Sultan, and I weep with him over his little granddaughter who faces surgery to remove a brain tumor. Your satellite pictures can never match that."

He was right.

The global, high-tech society needs local high-touch envoys of the Lord Jesus. Do you think Peter's witness, portrayed on television, would have impacted the persecutors the way his personal presence did?

Shortly before his death, the erudite, scholarly, and spiritual Bishop Chandu Ray of Pakistan made public a definitive survey of believers on the subcontinent. Forty-one percent (41%) came to Christ through a Christian explaining Bible passages to them face-to-face. Another 23 percent came to Christ through reading the Scripture. Fewer than 8 percent came to Christ through mass crusades, radio, or television.

Thank God for evangelistic crusades, and for all the high-tech media God uses to bring people to Himself. But the most effective communication, by huge multiples, is still found in high-touch — people to people, one on one. We can't reach people by remote control. We need to lead them — personally — to the power, presence, and proclamation of Jesus Christ.

That's what Haggai Institute, under God, has stood for all these years. It's what we still stand for.

Well, you don't need me to tell you that what one leader strives to gain, the next is afraid to lose. After pioneers develop a track record, the subsequent leadership often becomes conservative and protective. But timidity and self-protectiveness have no place in faith's behavior. Faith is neither timid nor self-protective. Faith dreams, and dares, and acts.

I have a motto:

Attempt something so great for God,

it's doomed to failure unless God be in it.

That's what the early trustees and supporters did. Today we have experience; we had none then. It was a high-risk undertaking with no manual of instruction. In the early days leadership got very little attention. Today it's a cottage industry.

Most of the trustees couldn't even identify the Third World on a map.

I had secured financial commitments in early 1969 to cover the costs of the first-ever seminar. Recession hit. Not one came through. We needed $99,800. On September 9, Pan Am gave us 24 hours to get them the money.

Carl Newton of San Antonio, Texas, phoned me

to say he had wired $100,000 (more than $600,000 in today's dollars). The news arrived six minutes before the deadline.

I had not asked Carl for any money.

The Lord had spoken to him.

Not for eighteen long years did we have money in hand before the start of any session.

Attempt something so great for God, it's doomed to failure unless God be in it.

The trustees stood fast, firm in faith. God bless their memory. Today, as I write, more than 7,000 national leaders serve the Lord in Asia, trained by those first 19 alumni.

Do you know the minimum dollar cost for supporting 7,000 American missionaries in those areas? First of all they can't get unrestricted visas — but if they could, it would cost $350 million every year. Makes the Haggai Institute costs look pretty good, doesn't it?

He who sees the invisible can do the impossible. Do you believe it? A group of daring believers back in the 1960s believed it.

Forever

God has given us a vision defining the future. What do we do about it — now?

Here are some questions for you:

Australia's population numbers around 20 million. Do you think Australia is over-evangelized? Do you think it has too many churches, too many seminaries? Too many Bible colleges? Too many Christian broadcasts and telecasts? Too many Christian bookstores? Too many Christian publication houses? Too many pastors and youth workers and musicians and theologians?

Do you know the population of India increases each year by more than the total population of Australia? If you believe Australia is not over-evangelized, then you must conclude that every 12 months all its Christian personnel, agencies, schools, churches, and institutions should be replicated in India.

Does that get to you? How sensitive are you to our Lord's Great Commission to resonate with that reality? Well, the same goes for China, whose population exceeds that of India.

I'm calling on you to renew your commitment to our Lord and His priority command.

Remember that command has two parts.

First, the action: Make disciples (Matthew). Preach the Gospel (Mark). Preach repentance and remission of sins (Luke). Witness (Acts).

That's only one part. Scripture warns us about adding to or taking away any words from the Bible.

Now, what's the second part?

The second part focuses on the area of action. All nations (Matthew). Every creature (Mark). Beginning at Jerusalem to the ends of the earth (Luke). The whole world (John). Jerusalem, Judea, Samaria, and the uttermost parts of the earth (Acts).

Do you have the vision?

Will you respond in faith validated by action?

Will you spend time every day praying for world evangelism — not generally, but specifically?

Will you invest your influence to recruit others to get involved? Will you sacrifice?

In 1996, I introduced a young man in our audience to the person most commentators consider the world's greatest futures trader. This man had turned an MIT classmate's 1972 $5,000 investment into $15 million by 1988. The globally famous trader turned to my young friend at the Everest House Restaurant in Chicago's financial center and barked, "Why do you want to make millions? You come from wealth. Why do you need money?"

The young man, then barely 25, looked at him with a steady gaze. He said, "I'm a Christian. I believe the Bible. The Bible says the most important work for any Christian is to spread the Gospel to the whole world. I think Haggai Institute does the best job at this. I want to make enough money so that Haggai Institute will never again walk away from an open door of opportunity for lack of funds."

Oh, and by the way, pastors, this young man puts his tithe in his church.

In America, we have one ordained senior pastor for every 506 Americans. In Asia, there's only one full-time Christian worker for every 614,000! Is that honoring to God? Does that reflect obedience to our Lord's Great Command?

By the grace of God, this ministry will continue to grow. That's not the issue. The issue is this: What part is God leading you to have in the great task of world evangelism? Where does our Lord's priority rest in your list of priorities? Can you really expect our Lord's optimum blessing on your life and work if His priority is not your priority?

I challenge you to show the same faith in this matter that you show when starting up a business, or making an investment, or underwriting your child's university education. Step out in faith. Attempt the impossible.

Impossible is the whole point.

But be careful what you call impossible!

4
YOU CAN'T SAVE TOMORROW

D r. Luke's recorded words of Paul in Acts 13:36-37 have haunted me for decades:

For when David had served God's purpose
in his own generation, he fell asleep; he was
buried with his fathers and his body decayed.
But the One whom God raised from the dead
did not see decay.

Now read what our Lord says:

But you are not to be like that. Instead,
the greatest among you should be like the
youngest, and the one who rules like the one
who serves. For who is greater, the one who
is at the table or the one who serves? Is it not
the one who is at the table? But I am among
you as one who serves (Luke 22:26-27).

Dr. Luke shows Christ as superior to David. David, great as he was, accomplished as he was, serving the Lord with effectiveness, "fell asleep." He died. His body saw corruption. It decomposed. David could serve only his generation.

Christ saw no corruption. He rose again. He serves all generations. He is God. We aren't — but we can do as David did and serve our generation.

It seems to me that the attitude of the average Christian does not impel to this spirit of service. That's tragic and far less than the best God challenges us to be. As followers of Christ, committed to Him, He expects us to faithfully, even sacrificially, serve our generation.

On 32 occasions, God called David *"My servant"* or *"My servant, David."*

Jesus said, *"I am among you as He that serves."*

By the way, "deacon" means "servant." It comes from a word that can be translated "dust sweeper." Jesus is called a deacon in the New Testament. The New Testament also calls Paul a deacon.

How well I remember many years ago, as an impressionable teenager, seeing a retinue of the stellar luminaries in the galaxy of the evangelical sky, sitting across the lower platform of Moody Church in Chicago. The celebrated minister Dr. H. A. Ironside, who preached to 3,500 every Sunday morning and 2,800 every Sunday night for 21 years, hosted a symposium attended by 4,000. Instead of taking his place in the middle of that august assemblage, as a host would be expected, Ironside went over in the corner, picked up a little folding chair in the vestry, and sat down inconspicuously in the doorway.

God bless the man of inconspicuous service. Not he, one to jockey for the center place in a photograph. Not he, one to manipulate behind the scenes to get other people to organize a testimonial dinner on his behalf, which he funded so it would appear as a grass-roots swell of popular support.

Not he, one to self-promote. H.A. Ironside was as one who served!

I think of the Maclellan Foundation in Chattanooga. As responsible stewards, they sent one of their members, Jere Tipton, an eminent lawyer, all the way to Singapore to evaluate the Haggai Institute program. Since then, they have invested millions in nations they'll never visit for the benefit of people they do not know, but for whom Christ died. God did not call them to preach, but God did call them to serve. And for three decades they have invested their enormous expertise, time, and money to serve.

David served his generation. He could not serve the preceding generation. Only Christ could do that, for He is without beginning of days. David could not serve the subsequent generation. Only Christ can do that, for He is without end of years.

You can no more serve the next generation than you can serve the last generation. The unbridled credulity of otherwise sensible people, thinking they can control from the grave money left in their estate, astonishes me.

My heart sinks when I think of the billions of dollars currently underwriting secular humanism, atheism, civil disobedience, same-sex marriages, violence, professors like Thomas Altizer who said God was dead, and Timothy Leary of Harvard who recommended the use of LSD. Billions given by God-fearing people. It sickens any thought-full person.

These generous and compassionate donors

meant well. They didn't understand they could not serve the subsequent generations.

I am so committed to this fact that my will is arranged so as to distribute my estate within ten years after my death or my wife's, whoever is the last survivor.

How David served his own generation

Since you'll never find a fail-safe way to control your estate from the grave, you need to prayerfully determine the best possible course to distribute now as much as possible for the glory of God.

Candidly, my hope for the continued integrity of the Haggai Institute ministry lies in the commitment of young people who currently serve as trustees. They may have 30 to 60 years ahead of them.

God forbid that we as believers should deny in death what we have affirmed in life. That implies responsibility to remember the Lord's work in every believer's will.

That's not what I am focusing on here. I'm focusing on what we do now.

A man told me recently, "I'm leaving my estate to Christian causes." I rejoice in that. One thing he has in common with everybody else is that he is leaving his estate. He has no alternative. He must leave it. Thank God he is leaving it to Christian causes.

I repeat, you can no more serve the next

generation than you can serve the last generation, except as the Holy Spirit, using your influence by life and by lip, induces family, friends, or associates to carry on your own vision and commitment.

David served his generation *"by the will of God"* (Acts 13:36). What are you doing about your generation? "Oh," you say, "I am no David." But God gives you capacity and ability just as He did David. Too often, it seems that we are saluting the cult of the comfortable and convenient. It seems that we are signing a treaty with the mediocre and — even worse — the minimal and marginal.

First, David served God in spite of his human inadequacy

When he prepared to fight Goliath, even those who should have stood by him — his own family — mocked him and made fun of him. They said, "Why don't you go back to the fields from which you came to take care of the sheep?"

In 1 Samuel 16, we learn that God sent Samuel to anoint as king of Israel one of the sons of Jesse. When Samuel saw Eliab, David's older brother, the Lord said to Samuel, *"Do not look at his appearance or at the height of his stature, because I have rejected him. God sees not as man sees, for man looks at the outward appearance, but the Lord looks at the heart."*

Then Jesse called his next son, Abinadab; then the next, Shammah. Jesse made seven of his sons to pass before Samuel.

Samuel said to Jesse, "The Lord has not chosen these." Then he asked, "Are these all the children?"

Jesse said, "There remains yet the youngest, and behold he is tending the sheep."

Samuel told Jesse to bring him, "For we will not move until he arrives."

When David came, the Lord told Samuel, "Arise, anoint him, for this is he."

Surely David felt inadequate standing by his older, big brothers.

Do you feel inadequate? Don't. You, too, can serve God — by serving your generation.

George Whitefield suffered a terrific speech impediment, and yet God made him the greatest orator in the English-speaking world, according to Charles Spurgeon. George Whitefield served his generation.

God took Dr. Kyung Chik Han from a sanatorium where he was suffering terminal tuberculosis, healed him, and made him a global statesman for Christ in spite of his human inadequacy.

Are you suffering human limitation, human inadequacy, psychological hang-ups, emotional hurts, physical debility? Do you feel inadequate? Don't. You, too, can serve God by serving your generation.

Mrs. Charles Spurgeon gave birth to twins. It nearly cost her life. She never fully recovered. An invalid the rest of her life, she nevertheless served God. She believed the world needed access to her husband's sermons. She had special concern for the poor preachers who couldn't afford commentaries.

She believed they should have his sermons. She engineered the entire program to raise funds, put the sermons in books, and distribute them to ministers across the world. Mrs. Spurgeon served God.

Second, David served God in spite of heinous iniquity

David served God even though he almost derailed himself with sin.

What a black page in the book of David's life. He became rich and indolent — a lazy, fat cat. He stayed home from battle when he should have been out fighting.

While he relaxed at home, he saw Bathsheba. Lust inflamed him. He committed adultery with her. He then arranged for the murder of her husband. And finally, to cover up his wickedness, he lied about the whole thing.

But God would not leave him alone. He sent Nathan the prophet to expose David's sin. David confessed his sin. He repented.

While he had not lost his salvation, he had lost the joy of his salvation. His repentance became as well-known as his sin. Out of that repentance came Psalms 32 and 51. How wonderfully God used him.

Do you feel that the reason you cannot serve God is because of some black mark in the diary of your past? Because of some smudge or some stain? Some horrible moral lapse? Something that you would to God you could obliterate? Ah, there is hope.

*If we confess our sins, He is faithful and just
to forgive us our sins and to cleanse us from
all unrighteousness* (1 John 1:9).

And while it is true that certain doors may be
closed because natural law goes on despite forgiven
sin, yet God can use you as He used David.

Third, David served God in spite of hostile opposition

David served God in the face of hostility.

Saul was arrayed against him; Saul tried to kill
David. He hounded David like a wild animal in the
caves of En-gedi and among the rocks of the wild
goats (see 1 Samuel 24:2).

Saul should have supported David. He should
have gone to any extreme to help him. David had
saved Saul's life. David had brought Saul out of his
foul moods with his masterful playing of the harp.
When David could have killed Saul, he spared
him. In fact, he cut a piece off his robe while Saul
was sleeping to convince Saul he had no ill will
toward him.

I know children from actively Christian homes
who felt called to serve the Lord on the mission field
or in the pastorate or in some ancillary ministry, but
their parents said, in effect, "You need not go into
the full-time ministry. You can serve God from a
prestigious secular position."

On the other hand, I've known children who

tried to manipulate and even intimidate their parents about their giving. The children feel that anything the parents give will detract from their inheritance. Poor dears. Poor slaves of a common American malady — the spirit of victimization. They don't seem to understand that in giving, the parents will have more, not less. Just as in sowing, the seed becomes more, not less.

These misled children look upon their parents' wealth as a huge pie. They erroneously believe that the bigger the piece of pie the parents give, the smaller the pie they will inherit.

They have trapped themselves in the wrong metaphor. It's not pie; it's seed. The more the parents sow, the larger the harvest the children will enjoy.

David's generation and ours

David served his generation. Are we concerned about this generation? It is worth examining your attitude.

Are you aware of the fact that the population of this world is increasing by more than 130 million births every year? Yet, according to statistician David Barrett, the total number joining all of the churches, including Jehovah's Witnesses, Mormon, Christian Scientist, Roman Catholic, Protestant, Orthodox, MarThoma, and Coptic, is less than 30 million. That means every year a net deficit, as far as the Kingdom of God is concerned, of more than 100 million people. In other words, 100 million more lost people are destined for Hell today than twelve months ago.

Does that concern you? Does it grieve you that hundreds of millions in China have yet to hear the Gospel of Jesus Christ? Do you mourn that only 3 percent of India's 1.1 billion claim Christianity as their religion, and of those, only 10 percent enjoy a personal relationship with the Lord Jesus? Do you lament the doors are closed in areas like Afghanistan, North Korea, and much of the Arab world?

Now, Jesus explicitly said that we are to evangelize all nations. What are you doing about this? The methodology obviously must change. We must come up with new methods. You say, "But how can we go where doors are closed?"

God has brought us to the conclusion that only new methods can meet today's challenge.

Here is a personal question. Do you believe that Jesus Christ, who loves you, would require of you that which is impossible for you to do?

Is not our Lord's command to us to go into all the world also His oath that the command can be fulfilled?

The question arises, "How can we get the Gospel to areas closed to Western missions?" The Western missionary can no longer get into these areas.

For instance, no Western preaching missionary can get a residence visa in India. With enough subterfuge, one may go in as a vocational missionary, but not as a preaching missionary. A preaching missionary is increasingly restricted in many areas of the world. And even while he may go to a place like Kuwait, he can't deal with the nationals — he's restricted to the expatriates.

That explains the "why" of the Haggai Institute strategy. Credentialed leaders come to Singapore and to Maui for advanced leadership training FOR EVANGELISM. They train in the "how" of evangelization. After they return, they transfer their training to their peer group, as they themselves do the work of evangelizing.

These nationals don't need a visa; they are already there. They don't have to learn the language; they already know it. They don't need to become sensitive to the culture; they already belong to it.

I don't know precisely how God will lead you. You may rest on a basic fact: He will lead you to serve your generation, and He will lead you to go global.

David served his day and generation by the will of God. He did it by serving others.

David served by his testimony. He said, *"Let the redeemed of the Lord say so"* (Psalm 107:2). After he'd told about God's glorious forgiveness, he said, *"Now, I can teach transgressors Thy ways"* (Psalm 51:13). And while that does not excuse his horrible sin, yet, by his testimony, he served.

David served with his talent. More than three centuries ago, the Scottish politician Andrew Fletcher wrote, "Let me write the songs of a nation and I care not who makes its laws." Well, David wrote their songs as well as administering their laws.

He served with his talent.

David served the Lord with his treasures. Did you know the temple of Solomon, in terms of today's gold value and the value of the other temple components, would cost over $13 billion? And did you know that David put more than $1.6 billion of his own money, according to today's standard, into that temple?

Frequently, when meeting with groups of high-income Christian executives, I ask: "How many of you men, at one time or another, really felt that maybe God was calling you to be a minister of the Gospel or to serve Him on the foreign fields?" Not once have I had fewer than 60 percent answer in the affirmative. Usually, it is 70 to 80 percent.

"Then," I say, "I want to ask a question. How can you be satisfied to give a mere tenth of your income to the Lord's work? Even the Jews did more than that. You were considering going into the Lord's service, where you never would have been able to amass your multimillion-dollar fortunes. Don't you think you ought to be honoring the Lord with this treasure, and instead of thinking in terms of a legalistic 10 percent, you ought to be putting in 20 or 30 or 40 percent or more?"

The late Guy Rutland told me that when he graduated from Georgia Tech he set a goal to make $1 million a year. "When I made the million dollars, I thought, 'That's not so great. I want to do something better with my life than this.'"

He gave more money every year than the 50 percent for which the U.S. government grants deductibility. He lived modestly. He could have lived grandly, enjoyed his own yacht, sailed the seven seas. Instead, he chose to serve God by serving his generation through his treasure.

Can we follow David?

God revealed Himself to David. David followed the leading of His eye. God used him to bless His world.

I don't know how God wants you to serve Him, but I suggest that you begin now with what you have, where you are.

How about putting the Lord Jesus in the middle of your social calendar? How about inconveniencing yourself, if necessary, in order to honor Him? How about taking some time out to read what's going on in the world so you can pray effectively?

How about putting Christ in the middle of your checkbook? Do your check stubs show that you honor Him? And what percentage of those check stubs would indicate that you're interested in the people who are not of your nationality?

Has it ever occurred to you that the people who are in the greatest need of prayer are those who do not know even to ask for prayer? If I carry a great burden, I can go to my friend, Dr. Bill Hinson, and say, "Bill, please ask our friends to pray for me." And he will pray for me. So will my brothers and sisters in Christ here and across the world.

But what about the person in China or Afghanistan or North Korea or Mindanao in the Philippines or Iraq or the Arabian Gulf? What about that man who is in great need? Many times he doesn't even know there is a God who loves him and who will answer prayer.

Only the Gospel of Jesus Christ reveals a God who loves. Islam does not reveal a God who loves. Buddhism does not reveal a God who loves. Hinduism does not reveal a God who loves. The same with Taoism and other religions. None of these faiths reveals a God who loves. Only the Gospel of Jesus Christ does that.

Has it occurred to you that the people who are in the greatest need are the ones we pray for the least? Has it occurred to you that 85 percent of the billions in the non-Christian world are off-limits to the Western missionary? Has it occurred to you that about two billion people in this world don't have a near neighbor to tell them about Jesus?

I think of Dr. John R. Mott, a layman — not a minister — who committed his life to making known the Gospel of Christ. He set up the YMCA in 300 cities, back when it was one of the great evangelistic agencies of the world. From 1895 until 1932, this man raised single-handedly, on six continents, $300 million for the work of the Lord. That would be like $6 billion today. He recruited 246,000 for Christian work. God used him to change the complexion of many areas of the world. And I say, "Oh, God, raise up some more John Motts."

I think of David Livingstone's servant who went to the great man's tent and saw him on his knees in prayer. He quietly exited the tent, not wanting to disturb him. The servant returned a little later. Livingstone was still in the posture of prayer, so again the servant left. When the servant came the third time, he touched Livingstone and realized that he had "fallen asleep."

He had died in the grandest and mightiest posture a man ever takes — on his knees. He had served God by serving his generation. Livingstone opened up the great continent of Africa. You cannot explain some of the work of God in Africa today apart from what God did through Livingstone.

What are you permitting God to do through you? What are you doing with your life? When you and I stand before God, we will want to say, "Not because of my worthiness or goodness, but because I was obedient and willing to let You work through me, here is what I lay at Your feet as a trophy of my service to my generation."

The reason we are committed to this program is that we have a distinct directive from Jesus, and that is to carry the Gospel to the ends of the earth. Are you willing to inconvenience yourself to cooperate in this globe-encircling endeavor to make Christ known?

When Jesus came to Golgotha,
they nailed Him to a tree.
They drove great nails through hands and feet
and made a calvary.

They crowned Him with a crown of thorns,
red were His wounds and deep,

For those were crude and cruel days,
and human flesh was cheap.

When Jesus came to our town,
they simply passed him by,
They never hurt a hair of Him,
they only let Him die.

For men had grown more tender,
and they would not give Him pain.
They only passed on down the street,
and left Him in the rain.

Still Jesus cried, "Forgive them,
for they know not what they do."
And still it rained that bitter rain that
drenched Him through and through.

The crowds went home and left the streets
without a soul to see,
And Jesus crouched against
a wall and cried for Calvary.
　　　　—Geoffrey Studdert Kennedy

God deliver us from apathy. Resurrect us, O Lord, from the tomb of complacency and convenience. So motivate us that we shall serve our day and generation by the will of God.

My one wish, personally, as I hope it is yours, is not to antagonize my generation, not to damage my generation, not to manipulate my generation, not to rule my generation, but to serve my generation by the will of God. I trust that is your priority. We do it with our testimony, our talents, our treasure.

Remember, God never moved the world through a majority. Rather, the creative and dedicated minority.

There is enough spiritual potential among the people reading this book, under God, to change this world for good. The decision is mine. The decision is yours.

5
EVERYTHING JUST CHANGED

I'm too old and too busy to play games, so I propose to cut through all the popular platitudes. I propose to relay to you the realities as I have learned them. My conclusions derive from a hundred trips around the world, plus many intercontinental journeys, plus days and weeks in the homes of Asians and visits of Asians in my home.

At his installation as president of the Baptist World Alliance in 1975, Hong Kong layman David Y. K. Wong said, "More of the same is not the answer." He was referring to the methods of global missions.

It's even truer today.

In 1997, news of the death of Princess Diana girdled the globe in two minutes. The news of the death of Jesus Christ still hasn't made it after 2,000 years!

So what to do? Do we cover ourselves with a warm sense of virtue and say, "Oh, it's sad. We tried so hard to get the message of God's redeeming love through Christ to the whole world, but the doors are closed."

Who said they are closed? If one door is closed, try another one.

If a team is losing games, you change the game plans, don't you? If a business is losing money, you change your business plan, don't you? Ask American Express, IBM, or General Electric. They have changed their game plans. And the words now are "from good to great" and "reengineering."

But the majority of Western believers insist on a now discredited method of world evangelism. The methods valid 100 years ago don't meet today's challenge.

I keep repeating: "The Message is changeless; the methods must change." I do no violence to the sweep of Christ's teachings when I remind believers, especially ministers and church leaders, of our Lord's words to the Pharisees about *"making the Word of God to none effect through your traditions"* (Mark 7:13).

A century ago, men wore celluloid collars, and women wore high-button shoes. Today such apparel would excite derisive laughter. The change in style does not obviate the need for appropriate clothing.

Consider current church mission budgets. The allocation of moneys for missions in Asia, for instance, has dwindled to a level that must grieve the heart of God.

True, many church leaders agree theoretically that new methods must be employed. More specifically, they realize nationals must reach nationals — or they won't be reached. But do they act on this premise? How many churches do you know who will support what they cannot dominate? Perhaps their support of the Bible Society is the exception that proves the rule.

How many mega-churches do you know who give as much as 15 percent of their budgets to reach the unevangelized through nationals? And how many churches do you know who are reaching the unevangelized in the Islamic nations and in the vast populations of non-Christian countries? And remember, when I say the unevangelized, I do not mean the expatriates.

Let's be clear.

You can make disciples; you can preach the Gospel; you can preach repentance and remission of sins; and you can witness — and still not obey the Great Commission.

Do you take seriously the command of Scripture not to add or subtract any words?

Somebody says, "You know, I have a tract ministry at the bus depot." God bless them. My mother had one, and that's fine. But that is not carrying out the Great Commission. You say, "Well, you know, I have a ministry in the marketplace." Well, that's fine. Praise God. But that is not carrying out the Great Commission.

Why? Because, as I said right at the beginning, the Great Commission is in two parts. I just alluded to one part: the function. The other half of the Great Commission relates to the area of function:

- "Make disciples of all nations."
- "Preach the Gospel to every creature."
- "Preach repentance and remission of

sins, beginning at Jerusalem, to the uttermost parts of the earth."

Jesus says, *"As My Father has sent me..."* Where? To the world. *"So send I you."* Where? To the world.

The most persistent command of God in the Word of God to the people of God is to evangelize the world. And yet our obedience to that command is muted, because we do not see clearly what is going on outside our own nation.

Here are some misconceptions we need to clear up — and quickly.

It's a myth that American mission-minded evangelicals understand the non-West

You can't trust the press — secular or religious — for an accurate portrayal of the global realities.

Most Westerners don't even know the facts. It's not their fault. The facts are obscured and even amended.

In 1987, the editor of *Christian History*, a Ph.D. from Boston College, read an article I wrote about slanted news. I said, "We talk about a slanted secular press, but our religious press is just as slanted. We don't report on ministries unless they are organically connected to an American ministry or American personnel. That is, unless it's so big — like David Yonggi Cho's 850,000-member church — that you can't ignore it."

This editor phoned me. He said, "I was so furious

when I read your article; I was prepared to rebut. But I did some research — and you're right."

Are you aware of the fact that God is doing a great work in Singapore — where about 76 percent of the people are Chinese (mostly Buddhists) and only about 18 percent are Christian? Yet half of the cabinet members are Christians.

Have you read about a Haggai Institute Indonesian alumnus whose church has grown from 20 members to 50,000 members in 18 years? They have built a 20,000-seat auditorium and a ten-story training center, all with Indonesian money. He's baptizing each month between 500 and 600 Muslims who have come to Christ.

Westerners filter the data through a distorted Western grid.

How many of those who pontificate about the conditions in China have been hosted in Chinese homes by Chinese people on their social, educational, and cultural level? They are hosted in clubs, hotels, and restaurants. How well do you get to know people whom you've never visited in their own surroundings or they in yours?

Over the years, I've spent days and weeks in Asian homes, and they have spent time in my home.

Intimate friends in the Far East, non-Japanese, have said, "America never would have dropped the atomic bomb on Berlin." I thought — and I still think — they were wrong, but perceptions are often more powerful than facts.

In early February 1999, in Scottsdale, Arizona,

I lunched with Dr. Dan Yeary, senior minister of Arizona's largest church. He told me that in 1962 the University of Tokyo invited him to address the faculty and graduate students, after which he would answer questions.

The address went well; the question-and-answer period did not. One of the graduate students said, "We understand why you dropped the first bomb. Why did you drop the second? You had won the victory."

Yeary told them he was not privy to military strategy and begged off. The student continued, "You never would have dropped the bomb on Berlin; it's your heritage."

I'm not debating the truth or falsehood of that matter. I am simply telling you, most Westerners do NOT understand the non-West. That's one reason why the most effective evangelist is a fellow national.

Coca-Cola understands that. IBM understands it. IGA understands it. The Western church just does not get it.

The cerebral 1969 Indonesian alumnus, Fred Thomas, said on Atlanta television, "You American Christians are willing to sacrifice your lives for us but not your thoughts; it's got to be done your way. And it's not working."

After dinner at our home in 1997, with Dr. and Mrs. Michael Youssef and the Egyptian Christian statesman Dr. Baki Sadaka, I took Michael aside to show him an article in one of my favorite magazines. It carried an article about an Egyptian Christian leader. I said to myself, "This will foment severe problems. It could mean danger for believers in Egypt."

Michael later that night showed the article to Baki Sadaka. Sadaka was appalled. The next day, Baki boarded a plane to attend a birthday party for Dr. Sam Habib, president of the Protestant churches of Egypt. After the party Baki showed Habib the article. Habib turned white. He knew this article could set back by many years God's work in the Middle East. Habib had worked tirelessly for decades to help Christian workers get visas. He valiantly worked for the body of Christ without fanfare, without announcement. No drum beating. This exposure could put an end to his effectiveness.

They went to their rooms. At 1:30 the next morning, Dr. Sam Habib suffered a heart attack. At 5:00 a.m. he was dead. Baki Sadaka, weeping, phoned Michael. Baki is not an emotional man. He bleeds inside, as I do, but like me, he has a hard time crying. He didn't even weep at the funeral of his beloved son.

Baki said, "Michael, it killed him."

Michael said, "No, no, no. You know, Baki, you are a great Bible scholar. *'It is appointed unto man once to die and after that the judgment'"* (Hebrews 9:27).

The author of the article, an eager reporter, who would gladly die for Christ, had no idea of the impact his article would have in the culture he was writing about.

It's a myth that the Asians look up to the United States with respect and envy

Americans champion democracy and freedom. Rightly so. But people in the non-West often see more clearly than we do what a price we pay to be free.

In Singapore, a brilliant, wealthy, highly placed leader, a professing Buddhist, probed me with questions.

"Is it true you have a problem with alcoholism in your country?"

I hesitated with my answer. He said, "I know for a fact that you have 11 million or more problem alcoholics. We have virtually none in Singapore."

He went on, "Is it not true you've got a big drug problem, in fact, the worst in history?"

This global savant, with two Ph.D.'s, didn't wait for my answer. He said, "The only drugs we have in Singapore are in the American and German embassies. Apparently they come in through the diplomatic pouches. Singapore hangs anyone found guilty of trafficking drugs."

He continued, "Is it not true that the United States is the most crime-ridden nation in the history of the world?" Again, he answered his own question. "Here in Singapore your wife or daughter would be safe walking unescorted on the street at 4:00 o'clock in the morning. Safer than she is in her American home with the burglar system armed."

He proceeded, "Is it not true that one of your major problems in America is juvenile rebellion against parental authority?" I had to concede.

He asked if pornography didn't plague America and perhaps incite criminal behavior. Then he said, "You know, of course, that this past year Singapore rejected 71 percent of Hollywood films sent over here as unfit for showing."

To further add to my embarrassment, he mentioned that America was now 38th in literacy in the world and that most Asian nations had higher literacy rates than the United States. And Canada. And Britain.

Then, looking me straight in the eye, he asked, "Exactly what are you doing over here? What have you to offer?"

I countered that we pay a heavy price for our freedom, but we prefer it to the alternative. It's true that man, when free, can create a ball and chain by which he imprisons himself — or create wings and soar.

It's a myth that the answer to world missions lies in sending more dedicated Western missionaries to unevangelized nations

In 1964, in Beirut, Lebanon, Christian men from the Arabic-speaking world met with me. They said,

"Tell your American friends to stop treating us like we are inferior."

I bristled. I said, "Let me tell you, I'm here because of the American missionaries. On average, one out of every four members of missionary families have died and been buried on Asian soil. What a price."

"No, no, no, *habibi*," they said. (*Habibi* is an Arabic term of great endearment.) "Don't get upset. But the truth is that people of high intellect and high position are not willing for foreigners to come over here, format the program, deploy the personnel, call the shots. We are better educated than they are. We know the Bible as well or better. We surely know Bible history better than they do."

Three days later, as if on cue, the heads of thirteen mission organizations, including my own denomination, honored me with a testimonial dinner. Grinning, they said, "Haggai, tell your camel-jockey cousins we can't hand everything over to them willy-nilly. We have to answer to our boards at 475 Riverside Drive, or in Richmond or Springfield, Nashville or Pasadena — wherever they may be."

I smiled wanly, but I was frustrated. They did not know about my previous conversation with the nationals. I thought, "What has happened? I'm savvy geopolitically. I'm well read. A group of researchers keeps me up to date. What has happened?"

And then it hit me. Of course! In the 19 years since World War II, a hundred new nations had been formed. Every Asian nation except Thailand

and Japan had been a colony in 1945. Now, with the independence, neo-nationalism emerged. These are sovereign nations.

Today, Syria is a sovereign nation. When my father fled from Syria in 1912, he said, "May I never see you again." At that time the Ottoman Empire in Turkey ruled Syria. It's a different story today.

Let's take the case of Bangladesh, a nation you hardly think about. In all probability you didn't pray for Bangladesh this morning.

To send missionaries to Bangladesh, in numbers matching the ratio of ministers to the U.S. population, we would need 260,000 missionaries, at a cost of $14.5 billion annually. That's four times our total current Western mission force and seven times our total annual mission income in all the Catholic and Protestant churches in North America.

To be blunt, it is economically impossible. And it's numerically impossible. And it's politically impossible. Bangladesh would never grant the visas.

And on top of all that, consider the impact of bringing Christianity to Bangladesh on the lips of Western missionaries.

Do you think a predominantly white American church would call a Chinese to be pastor, even if he were a seventh-generation American? No. My wife Christine will tell you that in 1946 a lady refused to rent us her apartment in that urbane university town of Greenville, South Carolina. Why? I was a foreigner. The lady frankly told me I was not acceptable.

My mother's people were English. On her maternal side, they settled in New England 120 years before the Declaration of Independence in 1776. One of my forbears, James Robinson, funded the Maine regiment during the Revolutionary War.

Yet my face reveals my Syrian background more than my English.

Why should the Asians be any more anxious to accept a Westerner than the Westerner is to accept them?

We are all ethnocentric.

It's a myth that the very structure of nondemocratic societies limits Christian outreach and spiritual blessings

Historically, God has done His greatest work in nondemocratic nations.

Over the centuries, the Holy Spirit has not been limited by political philosophy.

Reflect on the locales of Gospel activity and missions outreach over the last 2,000 years:

- Alexandria and Ephesus in the 2nd and 3rd centuries
- Constantinople, Turkey, from AD 330 to AD 600
- Rome from 600 to 1050
- France during the 12th, 13th, and 14th centuries

- Germany and Switzerland during the 15th and 16th centuries
- The Iberian Peninsula during the 16th and 17th centuries
- England during the 18th and 19th centuries

How many of these were democracies?

How many of them practiced free enterprise? Don't make the mistake of trying to confine God to a political box.

It's a myth that nationals lack the qualifications, know-how, and the inclination to evangelize their nations

There is not a word of truth to it.

Consider Dr. Won Sul Lee of Korea, secretary general of the International Association of University Presidents, a Ph.D. from Case Western, for years head of graduate studies at the 35,000-student Kyung Hee University in Seoul, and later university president in Taejon.

Or the late Benjamin Moraes who could read, write, and speak twelve languages. He authored more than 40 books. He built up the great Copacabana Presbyterian Church in Rio. He, the first-ever Protestant to be invited to serve as a cabinet minister, served under three Brazilian and Roman Catholic presidents. He wrote the penal code for Brazil.

Or the late Dr. Han Kyung Chik, schooled on both sides of the Pacific. His Princeton classmates selected him president during the dark days of America's Oriental Exclusion Act, when Orientals were excluded from becoming American citizens. This man founded colleges and middle schools and hospitals and orphanages. Dr. Han built a church from 27 refugees to 60,000 members with a $70 million budget. There's nothing like it in the United States. He established more than 500 churches, one of which is the Young Nak Church in Downey, California. In 21 years, it has become the third largest church on the West Coast.

Or the late Dr. Chandu Ray of Pakistan, the first Asian ever consecrated an Anglican Bishop. Before becoming Haggai Institute's faculty anchor person, he served as bishop of the Karachi diocese in Pakistan. Under God, he built it from 8,000 to 57,000 in 12 years, during which time he translated the Bible into two languages and had a million Muslim inquirers.

Or Dr. Anthony D'Souza of Bombay, a Jesuit who established the Indian Institute of Management and the Xavier Institute of Management. He has lectured on all six continents, showing leaders how to resolve conflicts and build winning teams.

In its 8 May 2006 issue, *Time* magazine listed Archbishop Peter Akinola of Nigeria, a Haggai Institute graduate, by the way, as one of the world's 100 most influential people. I suggest you read the article.

They are not qualified? Tell me where you are

going to find their equal in the city you live in.

Need I go on? I could fill several books with examples like these. And you are still saying nationals are not qualified to do the job in their country?

It's a myth that the non-Western, non-Christian nations lack the money to evangelize their people

Categorically wrong!

No church in this country has put the kind of money into missions as have some of the Asian churches.

Bombay has more millionaires than Chicago. This caveat: many Chicago millionaires are paper millionaires; Bombay millionaires are liquid.

Y. K. Pao, shortly before he died, wanted to buy the British, French, and Saudis out of their four-way consortium. He allegedly wrote a check for $23,400,000,000. Dick DeVos, then president of Amway, heard me make that statement. He said, "That's right. When I was a young man, Dad took me to meet Mr. Pao." I'm not sure Y. K. Pao ever made it on the *Forbes* or the *Fortune* lists!

God has put enough money in every nation to do everything He wants done in that nation. The money is all over the place. By all means read *The Mystery of Capital* by Hernando DeSoto for documentation that the above paragraph is true. This book has been endorsed by Walter B. Wriston, chairman emeritus, Citigroup; Jeane Kirkpatrick, former U.S. ambassador to the United Nations; Javier Pérez de Cuéllar, former secretary general of the United Nations; and Margaret Thatcher, former prime minister of the United Kingdom.

In 1983, I spoke in Bombay on Christian stewardship. During a question-and-answer time at the end, an Indian multimillionaire Christian businessman commented, "This will require some adjustment in my thinking. The missionaries taught us that our only obligation was to show up. They would provide the program, the building, and the funds."

During casual conversation, another Indian said to me, "There's plenty of money in India to evangelize India. Some of it's in my pocket. But why should I give when the West will pay the bills? We have the American church in India; we have the British church in India; we have the Canadian church in India; we have the Australian church in India; we have the German church in India; but we don't have the Indian church in India. And we never will until we start paying the bills." His name: Dan Souri of New Delhi.

Then why does Haggai Institute need funds?

First, many countries severely restrict what they permit their people to take out of the country. Second, some of the clergy we train have limited resources. One man sold his motorcycle, his only means of long-distance travel, to get together the $500 required of each participant. Another minister cashed in all of his savings and borrowed against his future salary.

But during the training they learn how to teach stewardship. They learn about the twin of soul-winning — money-winning. Today, the H.I. work in India and Brazil is self-supporting.

On average, each alumnus trains at least 100 others, so the donor's dollar does the work of $100 — and more. Underwriting one leader at a cost of $9,100 does the work of nearly $1 million!

What is God asking us to do?

I ask you two questions:

- Do you believe the Gospel is Good News? And,
- Do you believe news is information previously unknown?

My answer, as yours, is a resounding "YES!" to both.

If that be true, then I submit to you there are more than 1.8 billion — that's 1.8 thousand million — for whom there is no Gospel and for whom the death of Jesus Christ is meaningless!

Has the Lord commanded us to evangelize them? YES!

Can equipped national believers do the job? YES!

Will you help to equip these thousands of national leaders required to do the job — our Lord's priority mandate to His church?

You can be sure that no enterprise on the face of the earth gives you the opportunity to penetrate the unevangelized areas of the world that Haggai Institute affords you.

Not only am I an ordained minister of the Gospel, God has also made me a broker of opportunities, global investment opportunities with guaranteed dividends. Nothing like it has been seen before; nothing like it can be seen now anywhere else on earth.

Here's an experience which may help you understand where I am coming from.

Several years ago, I visited a prominent businessman, a Christian man, a good man. He had amassed tens of millions of dollars. By every worldly criterion, he was a success.

We had chatted briefly when he said, "John, I think you are doing good, and I want to help you out."

I replied, "Wait, w-w-wait; hold on; something has gone awry in this conversation. You want to do what? You want to help me out? No, no, no."

"Well, I know things are going well with you, but I know you can always use a little extra money."

Many times they will give you a nuisance check just to get rid of you. I was not going to let him off that easily.

I said, "You want to help me out? How? Give me a new suit? Recommend me for membership in a country club? How can you help me? I'm not here for me. Frankly, there is nothing you can do for me, though I appreciate your friendship. I know that you would give me a check. I don't want one. One day you are going to stand before God, and you are going to give an account for the people who could have been won to faith in Christ by Christian leaders trained, but who were not trained because you failed to do what God had enabled you to do."

He said, "Well, I've got relatives, each of whom I want to make a millionaire."

I interrupted, "Frankly, I did not come here to discuss the distribution of your estate. I came here to give you an opportunity to obey the Great Commission and touch lives in nations where the Gospel does not have much penetration."

I smiled, shook his hand, looked him deep in the eye and said, "Bill, you haven't begun to take seriously the most persistent command of God in the Word of God to the people of God. You have failed here — to your own detriment. This weighs most heavily upon the heart of God. As I leave, I am praying that God will lay your opportunity heavily upon you and that you will respond to it."

I left him. In my view, he still has not risen to his potential, but he has come a long way from where he was.

I am over 80 years old. Neither time nor culture nor personal financial needs nor workaholism drives me to do what I do. I take seriously the mandate to get the Gospel to the whole world. And if I am 100, I intend to use what strength I have to continue in that pursuit.

I cannot quantify precisely what your financial

commitment will accomplish. Only God knows that. I can quantify what it will provide in terms of people trained. I can tell you that we are now set up to train over 2,000 a year in our international sessions; the only drawback is funds and personnel. The personnel needs could be solved with adequate funding.

To be sure, we shall proceed. Thank God for people who are committed to the Great Commission, people who do not need the social cachet of some popular, name-recognized fad, people who will never get their names put on a bronze plaque, superimposed on the obelisk in the Town Square when they give to Haggai Institute. However, when you invest, you will be touching the world with the Gospel of Jesus Christ.

And I must tell you that I am not asking you to do anything I'm not doing. God has blessed us. He has blessed us in ways that would be incomprehensible to the average person. He has blessed us with the individual management of money so that I am able to give significantly to this ministry. That is beyond the 50 percent I give to my church and a half dozen select ministries.

True, it represents a large proportion.

I simply want you to know that I am not asking anybody to do anything that I'm not doing. And I want you to know, in a measure, the extent of my concern, the intensity of my passion.

If you knew you had only 30 more days to live, what would you do? What changes would you make? How would you reallocate your time — and your money?

Through Haggai Institute, you've got an opportunity to impact the world for Jesus Christ. It requires a humility that is rare—humility to support what you can no longer dominate.

As God provides additional millions of dollars, we will be able to do more publishing, fact-finding, data-gathering, and electronic communications to augment this ministry.

Bob Pierce, the founder of World Vision, phoned me just before he died. He said, "John, this afternoon I am telling the doctors to pull the plug on the life-support systems. I should be in Heaven within three or four days, but I want to talk to you while I still have my mental faculties. Turn on the recorder."

He then told of his passion and of his desire, above all things, whatever was done, whether it be in social service such as orphanages, world relief, assistance to the poor or whatever, that every dollar invested would carry with it the message of Christ's redeeming love.

I challenge you to ask yourself this question: What am I giving to, and is it eventuating in people coming to know the Lord Jesus Christ? Who gave us the money? Did the people to whom we are giving have anything to do with our developing the funds? Or did it come from God Almighty who gives us this opportunity and commands us to go into all the world and preach the Gospel?

Moses said to the Israelites, *"And you shall remember the LORD your God, for it is He who gives you power to get wealth"* (Deuteronomy 8:18).

Jerald Panos said, "Do you know what a poor organization is? A poor organization is an organization led by people who are not capable of realizing all the opportunities God puts in their hands."

As I write this, the waiting list bulges with more than 8,600 credentialed leaders from scores of nations. To say, "Yes" to them will require more than $73 million. The money is available; it only needs to be released.

In Arizona in early February 2000, I listened to Dr. William Hinson, the senior minister of Houston's First Methodist Church. He told a story that left us all misty-eyed.

He'd been a student at college, 18 years old. It was his second sermon at a very small rural Methodist church. A little barefoot boy in the front row kept swinging his feet back and forth. It so distracted Bill and finally mesmerized him that he had to conclude his message in eight minutes and dismiss the service. When the benediction had been offered, the little boy went up and said, "Gosh, you are a good preacher. Can you come and have dinner with us?"

Bill thought, "Well, at least they owe me that. He wrecked my sermon."

After he had dinner, the little fellow was all starry-eyed and totally enrapt by the young minister.

On Wednesday, Bill Hinson received a letter. It rattled. He opened it, and out fell fifty-seven cents in dimes, nickels, and pennies. The little fellow had sent the fifty-seven cents. His name was Donny Morris. He said, "This is my egg money. I'm going to help you get your education."

Finally, Bill was able to contact Donny's father and said he wanted to return the money and asked how he could go about it. Donny's father said, "Please, you can't do that. It will be a terrible thing for you to return the money. He is taking better care of those chickens than he ever has."

All through college and seminary, Donny Morris kept helping Bill Hinson. Then this gifted and dedicated pastor of Methodism's largest church in the United States said, "As I stand here, I can tell you that Donny Morris is paying the total expenses — including tuition, books, computers, room and board, travel — for 22 university students. Oh yes, and two years ago Donny Morris flew down to Houston in his private jet to check on his first investment."

God will not be anyone's debtor. Donny Morris may have given more sacrificially than any of us will. Whether that is true or not, ours is the opportunity to provide training for one gifted and potentially powerful world leader, and further, for literally tens of thousands of leaders in countries we may never visit, evangelizing people we will never meet this side of Heaven.

6
LEVERAGE YOUR RESOURCES

Excuses are easy.

Oh, you say, I don't have the resources; I don't have the money; I don't have the time; I don't have the right gifts.

Of course, you don't. God knows that. And God supplied a simple solution.

Archimedes said, "Give me the right lever, and I'll move the world."

Moses' father-in-law, Jethro, knew all about leverage. He watched Moses sitting in judgment, from dawn to dusk, over an endless stream of petty disputes. He saw the enormity of the work. He could see Moses faced burnout in trying to keep up with such a herculean task. And his advice was, "Use leverage. Go train a team of trustworthy men to serve as judges so only the hardest cases can reach the top."

In brief, use a defined strategic effort to achieve the optimum desired results. Those judges constituted the lever Moses used to crack the problem of settling the people's disputes.

You don't shift a big weight with a short lever. You find a long lever. You place the fulcrum close to the point of resistance, the thing you want to move; you get as far away from the fulcrum as you can, and you press the lever with all your might.

Dr. Michael Youssef could never have discipled the 150 who came to Christ under his Leading the Way ministry in Tunisia. It would have been physically impossible. But God provided the fulcrum and the lever.

A young man whom Dr. Youssef sent for Haggai Institute training at a Middle East seminar returned to Tunis in Tunisia where no missionary can work except with the expatriates — and even there it's difficult. He was perfectly positioned. Michael, on the end of a three-thousand-mile lever, exercised his special gifts of Gospel preaching and spirit-led leadership to equip his young Tunisian friend for the work of discipling others. That way, he met the needs of 150.

Michael could never have done it himself, any more than I could. Nobody in the United States could have fulfilled that ministry. Michael made a defined strategic effort to achieve the optimum desired result. Ponder the ways you can leverage your resources to change the world for good.

One: Leverage your time

Jesus said, *"I must work the works of Him that sent me while it is yet day, and night cometh when no man can work"* (John 9:4).

The Apostle said, *"Redeem the time"* — or buy it up, buy it back — *"for the days are evil"* (Ephesians 5:16). And again he said, *"Brethren, the time is short"* (1 Corinthians 7:29).

That's what he told the Corinthians.

Why do I add staff? To buy time. In my student pastorate, I engaged a very capable assistant pastor, my seventeen-year-old brother Tom, for which I paid him the princely sum of fifteen dollars a week.

Six hundred people resided in the 150 houses in Jackson, South Carolina. Tom and I did what we called the prayer-meeting blitz. Every Wednesday afternoon, the two of us knocked on every one of those 150 doors inviting people to come. He started from one end of the hamlet, and I from the other.

The prayer meeting attendance increased from an average of 7 to an average of 105! We leveraged our time. I could not have done it by myself, and Tom could not have done it by himself. Leveraging time made it possible.

In the early days of the Haggai Institute ministry, I personally selected nineteen people from four nations who attended the first seminar.

In the late sixties, I personally recruited the faculty: the renowned Dr. Han Kyung Chik of Korea, Dr. Chandu Ray of Pakistan, Dr. Fouad Accad of Lebanon, Dr. Max Atienza of the Philippines, and world Christian statesman Dr. Ernest Watson of Australia. I could have continued in that role. I could be doing the work that my executive staff members do. But it would not be done as well, and the resulting time limitation would have so restricted us that instead of having over 65,500 graduates, we would be fortunate to have 6000.

Over the years, by the grace of God, I've tried to recruit capable staff in order to buy time and accomplish more — defined strategic effort to achieve the optimum desired result.

John Bolten, our German-American trustee, traveled with me on an around-the-world missionary journey. In Korea, I preached for my friend Dr. Cho who built the world's largest church — 850,000 members. They pack it out nine times on Saturday night and Sunday, with 50,000 at each service. After the service, John said, "That must have been a great thrill. You must really miss the pastorate. What an opportunity this has been for you to once again feel the challenge of the local church pulpit."

I said, "John, what are you trying to tell me? How many of the 50,000 people present today do you think never heard the Gospel before?"

"Well, I guess I don't know."

"Well, I can tell you. At the very most, 3 percent — 1,500 people. As it is" — and this was back many years ago — "Haggai Institute now has 4,400 alumni. Suppose, on average, each has presented the Lord Jesus and the message of salvation this week to ten who have never heard the Gospel. He said, "It's far more; I've seen what they are doing. It would be at least ten times that number."

"If so, John, that's 440,000," I said. "How could I possibly be overjoyed at turning my back on a possibility like that, even if all 1,500 unbelievers here today came to Christ?"

In 1965, I read a statement written in the 1800s by John Morley: "He who does the work is not so profitably employed as he who multiplies the doers." It rocked me in my socks.

Today, over 65,500 alumni are taking the Gospel to millions in 178 nations. That's leverage.

During this past year, how many people have you told about Jesus Christ and explained the plan of salvation for the first time? By involvement in this program, you leverage your time to reach millions — millions neither you nor your church could reach in a lifetime — because Haggai Institute leverages time through personnel.

Haggai Institute is not dependent on John Edmund Haggai. I could drop dead right now; the trustees could dissolve the organization, and the 65,500 trained leaders would keep it going for fifty or a hundred years — who knows how many! I don't know of any other enterprise, spiritual or secular, including General Electric, Toyota, or Siemens, whose personnel make the chairman nonessential to its continuity.

But one day you're going to stand before Jesus Christ and He's going to say, "How many more could have heard the Gospel if you had done what you were capable of doing?"

Two: Leverage your relationships

In 1965, I met a young man whose mini-biography I had read a few months earlier in the *Atlanta* magazine. I made a note to arrange a meeting with him. Miraculously, without any effort on my part, I met Hank McCamish in February of 1965, in his magnificent office on the top floor of Atlanta's Bank South building.

Hank accepted the invitation to become one of our earliest trustees. In 1976, Hank introduced me to Polly Poole. In 1981, Polly Poole introduced me to Ralph Doudera. In 1997, Ralph Doudera introduced me to one of his business colleagues in the Midwest.

Collectively, these men have given multiplied millions to evangelize the great Asian areas. More than 60 percent of the world's people live in Asia. Yet less than 25 percent of the total mission forces of America — Canada and the U.S. — minister there. Neither China nor India, with their combined population exceeding 2.25 billion, grant unrestricted preaching missionary visas to any Western missionary.

Each of these men has traveled with me around the world to determine firsthand the validity and effectiveness of the H.I. ministry. In obedience to our Lord's command, each has leveraged his time and relationships for spreading the Gospel to the ends of the earth.

I repeat: The formula for effectiveness in world evangelism can be summed up as a defined strategic effort made to achieve the optimum desired result.

Third: Leverage your prayer power

Pray, but also enlist others to pray.

The great Lyman Beecher, who built the fabulous Park Street Congregational Church in Boston, which you've seen as a historical marker off the Boston Common, was asked, "How do you have such incredible success?" He said, "Every Sunday morning when I am preaching, four hundred of my laymen are in the lower auditorium on the knees of prayer, beseeching the God of the universe to do great and mighty things."

In 1969, I conducted a citywide meeting in Beirut, Lebanon. One of the Middle East's more effective evangelists, Rev. Maurice Girgis, whom I had never met, heard about the meeting. He cancelled his own meetings. He fasted and he prayed during the entire week.

He believed I was surrounded by a horde of theological liberals, but he was glad I was preaching the Gospel. He was confident I would not compromise. He prayed that the Holy Spirit would endue me with power. He prayed many would come to a saving knowledge of Jesus Christ. God honored his ceaseless intercessions.

I believe that was the last citywide appeal for souls prior to the fall of Beirut. Girgis recruited others to pray. Over the years Girgis had taught his fellow Christians in the Middle East to pray. How he leveraged his prayer power!

Charles Spurgeon declared, "I'd rather teach one man to pray than ten men to preach."

Defined strategic effort made to achieve the optimum desired result.

Four: Leverage your information base

In 1968, I met Roy Robertson, one of the twentieth century's exceptional missionary statesmen. He earned a reputation as a flying ace in World War II.

He set records in the automobile business in Dallas after the war. Then the Lord did a work of grace in his heart. He joined the Navigators. They sent him to China. He buried a wife and two babies while ministering in that great land. When people asked him why he didn't come back to the States, he said, "Why should I? My heart is in Asia."

Understandably, the Asians love him. They trust him. He set up my citywide evangelistic campaigns in Jakarta in 1968.

One day I said, "Roy, what is it with you? How is it that everything you do, you do with such skill — with such victorious results?"

He said, "To God be the glory!"

I said, "That's fine. I understand that. But tell me what it is that makes you do it. A lot of people give God the glory."

He said, "Years ago, a man told me that a genius is always at the mercy of a man of mediocre intelligence but with superior information."

That statement changed my life. From that day, I determined to acquire the best information available — whether it's medicine, whether it's finance, whether it's missiology.

Many people here and across the world "ghost read" for me, for instance. They understand my mind-set — which takes a miracle. They know what I'm looking for. Others get inside information to me regarding geopolitical, demographic, cultural, and religious changes.

Leveraging.

We knew about the fall of Ethiopia to the Communists in the early 1970s before the foreign affairs ministries of the world or the U.S. State Department knew about it.

I phoned H.I.'s dean, Dr. Ernest Watson, to put our Ethiopian man on the very next plane. He arrived back in Addis Ababa just in the nick of time. He later told me that if he hadn't been on that plane he would have been put in jail and maybe killed.

Effective prayer requires adequate information. What does the Apostle Paul tell us through Timothy? Read it carefully and repeatedly:

> *I exhort therefore, that, first of all, supplications, prayers, intercessions, and giving of thanks, be made for all men; for kings, and for all that are in authority; that we may lead a quiet and peaceable life in all godliness and honesty* (1 Timothy 2:1-2).

How can you pray for people you don't even know exist? Do you know the names of *"all that are in authority"* in the world's more than 200 nations? I have not yet met the person in the West who can give me the names of even 13 Third World heads of state.

We have an obligation to know the situation. We should be aware that people are not starving today because of inadequate food supply. There's enough food — and I don't mean potential — to give every person on the planet three square meals a day, but it's being hoarded.

Are you old enough to remember the Live Aid concert where some Western celebrities raised $70 million to alleviate the suffering and forestall the imminent death of the starving Ethiopians?

Do you know the result? A knowledgeable African leader told me, on condition of anonymity, that crooked and heartless political leaders confiscated those millions. They used the money to persecute the very people it had been raised to help. They debased it into a political tool to create carnage and death for innocent citizens.

I applaud the gallant motivation and masterful "generalship" of Sir Robert Geldof in recruiting world celebrities to take part in this noble effort.

But feeding the hungry of the world requires more than food; it requires a change in the heart of man.

Did you know that past Vice President of Zambia, General Godfrey Miyanda, a Haggai Institute graduate, extends his influence throughout Zambia and on much of the African continent? He served on the cabinet of the President as Minister of Education.

Or that at one time, three Haggai Institute alumni ran for the presidency of their respective countries? Or that an H.I. alumnus, Reynato

S. Puno, has just been made Chief Justice of the Supreme Court for the Philippines.

The President of Nigeria, Olusegun Obasanjo, a believer, sent me an invitation by a Catholic priest who took our training. He said, "I've read all of Haggai's books. Tell him to come for a visit with me." I didn't take up the invitation — flattering as it was — because I needed to leverage my time.

In the last few paragraphs, I've given you information many of you have neither heard nor read. This information can help you leverage your resources to evangelize the world if you want to.

Defined strategic effort made to achieve the optimum desired result.

Five: Leverage your money

Can you imagine what $50 million poured into this ministry could have accomplished for the humanitarian benefit of the people in need, to say nothing of their spiritual enlightenment and salvation?

Professor of management Ruth Callanta of the Philippines has testified that since her training in Maui, she has already reached more than a hundred thousand (100,000) with the Gospel. Not only that, but as a leading professor she has worked with other Haggai Institute graduates to produce a clinic, a nutritional center, a school, an orphanage for the poorest of the poor, a water purification program, and micro-financing of micro-enterprises as an entry point for sharing the Gospel.

All of that was done with local funds — not one American dollar. Is that leveraging? The entire program eventuated from the sacrificial gift of one $9,100 sponsorship. Talk about the power of leverage.

To those well-meaning, but hesitant and skeptical Christians who fear they may waste their gift, I don't argue. I just remind them that our Lord never condemned a bad investment. He only condemned no investment.

When I was a boy, my father's salary amounted to $14 a week. I bought every suit I've ever had on my back since the time I was ten. When I was nine, I started selling the *Washington Observer*. I walked three miles every day to sell four newspapers. I made a penny a day per paper. That gave me 24 cents a week. I put 3 cents in the offering — that was more than my tithe. With some Christmas gifts I had received — one was 50 cents; two were for 25 cents — by and by, I bought a secondhand bicycle for $5.50 so I could go and hoe corn for 25 cents an afternoon after school.

I then moved into the world of commerce, scraped up every dime I could find, bought a hand-operated printing press and started making letterheads, envelopes, business invoices, and business cards.

My father nearly wept that he was unable to afford any kind of a gift the day of my graduation.

In 1969, I had gone through all of my savings

in trying to keep this ministry alive. That summer, the world's largest independent oil concessionaire, Dr. Wendell Phillips — you've read about him in the magazines, the *Wall Street Journal*, the *Financial Times*, and other business publications — phoned me from New York. He said, "I'll put a million dollars in your hand tomorrow if you'll give me twelve months of your time to help in the Middle East. We'll split the ORRI — the overriding royalty interest."

I declined.

He said, "What's the matter? Not enough money?"

I said, "Your job's too small."   (If I'd done it, it would have made me $37 million.)

When I hung up I thought, "What kind of a fool are you? Here is Johnny, our invalid son, with his enormous medical needs and their consequential costs. There's the help required to assist my wife Christine." I had just sold my car to make payroll.

Paul the Apostle said, "If you don't provide for your family, you've denied the faith; you're worse than an infidel!"

It was one of the bleakest days of my adult life. Nobody knew my plight — not even Christine. Though she said she knew things were tight, she didn't know how bad it was. Nobody knew. I didn't tell my closest colleagues. I didn't tell Phil Gordon. I didn't tell Harold Keown. I didn't tell Hank McCamish. Nobody knew. God saw me through in ways I will not divulge until you read them in my memoirs.

When I suggested to Chris in 2000 that she might want to give, above her tithe, $200,000 to this globe-encircling ministry, she began to weep. It grieved me. I thought I had offended her.

I said, "What's the matter? Have I upset you?"

She said, "Do you remember in our student pastorate in South Carolina I wrote a letter, and we could not get the pennies together to buy a postage stamp to send it to Bristol? How good God has been!"

When a man said to our CEO, Dr. William M. Hinson, "You'll have to understand, I really can't afford to tithe; we have heavy expenses," Bill let him know in no uncertain terms that what he said was falling on deaf ears. The Hinsons for years have given a double tithe, and frankly I do not know how they do what they do. Others close to them, who know their living habits, agree with me. They are not suffering.

Parenthetically, some reader may say, "Haggai is making a pitch for his own organization." If you think that, you don't understand the realities.

In 1949, when I pastored a church in Lancaster, South Carolina, did I stress missions? Did I stress money? You better believe it. The year before I was there, they gave $227 to missions. My first year there, the church budgeted $12,500 for missions out of the total $26,500 budget.

The same thing happened in Louisville. While there, the missions giving — it doesn't sound like much now, but this is more than half a century ago — went from $16,000 to $106,000.

I have poured my heart out on behalf of world evangelism for more than 60 years — on both sides of the pulpit.

In 1989, I told my confidants that I wanted out. I had given 43 years of nonstop effort, unrelieved by vacations or weekends off. I wanted out.

The Pope's personal representative, Fr. Dr. Anthony D'Souza, our senior faculty member, flew all the way from Tokyo to Singapore, to talk with me. He said, "Dr. Haggai, you cannot do it. It would strike a blow to the credibility of the organization. As long as Asians perceive you to be vigorous, they would never understand why you are backing out."

I hope I have made the point, I don't lead this ministry because I have no options. I lead it because of a Divine mandate and a sober reminder of that mandate through godly, thus sage, advice. I continue at 83 as a matter of personal privilege. I am here because I am passionately committed to getting the Gospel to the whole world.

America has given more money and more aid and more material assistance to the needy people of the world than all other nations combined. I applaud that. Also we are witnessing the establishment of thousands of charitable foundations in this country — foundations both private and public. That's good. But I hasten — as you would expect — to express a concern.

I was talking with a dear, dear friend. He has built a billion-dollar empire. He's a modest man. He does not like attention. He told me he'd put together a private foundation.

I said, "To what end?"

He looked at me puzzled and said, "To do good and underwrite Gospel programs and to help mission efforts."

I said, "How much of the corpus do you distribute each year?"

"Well, the required minimum — 6 percent."

I said, "God forbid, if you were to drop dead now, what assurance do you have that your wishes will be carried out?"

"Oh, I have a board of trustees. They'll carry out my wishes."

I said, "Really? Let me ask you some pertinent questions. How many trustees do you have?"

He said, "Nine."

"Who are they?"

"Well, people in whom I have confidence. I have people that I believe to be fine Christians."

I said, "How many of these people on your board of trustees would you invite into your corporate planning meetings to suggest actions to enhance and enlarge your business?"

He looked at me with a quizzical frown and said, "I don't know — maybe one."

"Another question: How much do these people give personally? For instance, is each of your trustees a tither?"

"Well, I don't know."

"You mean you are entrusting the distribution of the fortune God has given you to people whose personal stewardship you know nothing about?

"Let me ask you another question: How many of these trustees in the past year have given to the ministries that you have given to — ministries you consider a priority?"

"Well, I'm not sure anyone has."

I looked at him in disbelief. I said, "I asked if they are tithers — you don't know. I asked if they shared your priorities — you don't know."

"No," he said, "that would be impertinent for me to ask."

I said, "It would?"

Even though I've not requested it, my accountant — whom I consider brilliant beyond description — shows me his 1040 every year, and I know that he gives 28 percent of his income to Christian work.

I have arranged for him to have a big say in the distribution of the funds upon my Homegoing or Christine's Homegoing. I'll guarantee you one thing: nobody will get near the funds that God has entrusted to me unless he is a tither to his church; unless he gives generously above the tithe; unless he has proved that his priorities are in sync with my priorities; and unless he has given to the very things that I think are important. Otherwise, I would be abandoning God's leadership and my obedience in terms of all the material possessions God has given me.

John Wesley was a multimillionaire in today's terms. He wrote 371 books. He said, "If I have more than 40 pounds when I die, call me a thief and a liar." As he was dying, he said to his helper, "What do I have left?"

The helper said, "Two silver spoons."

Wesley told him, "Give them to the wife of Parson So-and-So."

"I'll do it. I'll do it."

Wesley smiled and said, "Now I can meet my Master with joy."

I realize that many from other countries don't get the deductibility that Americans and Canadians get for gifts made to God's work.

I tell you gently, that's no excuse not to give according to God's teachings. Many of you don't have the capital gains tax Americans and Canadians pay. In some instances you can buy a building for a million dollars, keep it for ten years, sell it for ten million, and you pocket the nine million tax free. One American friend of mine said in a jocular vein, "We'll swap our deductibility for your capital gains any day!"

In the final analysis, it's not what you don't have. Jesus didn't say, "Give — as long as it doesn't exceed your 50 percent tax limit — and it will be given to you in good measure, pressed down, shaken together."

One illustration. Our first chairman, J. I. "Mac" McCormick, underwrote the training of a brilliant nuclear medicine authority, Dr. George Samuel of Tiruvalla, India. Equipped with this training, George Samuel miraculously acquired seven acres of land in India. He developed a thriving banana and rubber business with local funds. He built an eleven-building campus, including an auditorium which accommodates 1,800, and a library of 14,000 volumes. Since 1973, he has trained over 8,500 leaders for evangelism.

No mission force in the West has ever grown to that size. Just one man. Talk about leverage.

The cost to fund that many missionaries in India today — you couldn't do it for that — would amount to $465,500,000 a year, every year, including the years the missionaries are on furlough. That's if you get unrestricted missionary visas, which you cannot.

As Mac was dying, he rejoiced in the many leaders he and wife Opal had trained. He didn't say to his aid, "Please bring my net worth statement and my stock certificates so I can lay my dying head upon them and get comfort." He didn't say, "Please bring the scrapbooks with all the clippings about my great achievements — and how many wonderful things people said about me — and all the wonderful awards and plaques." He didn't say that. No, he said, *"Not unto us, O Lord, not unto us, but to Thy name be glory."*

Years after his death, Mac McCormick continues to change the world because he leveraged the money God gave him.

My dad never made twenty thousand dollars a year in his life.

I'd go to the house and I'd be sweltering. I said, "Dad, you've got air conditioning. So turn on the air conditioner."

He said, "No, the fan is cheaper. Get in front of the fan."

I'd go there in the wintertime; I'd be freezing. I said, "Dad, you've got heat. Just set the thermostat higher."

"No, here's a sweater. It's much cheaper."

He would get a small dividend check and say, "Son, I want you to drive me to the bank so this will get interest over the weekend."

I said, "Dad, it's costing me more to go and pick

you up and take you to the bank than the interest you'll earn over the weekend."

With a twinkle he'd say, "Yes, but that's your money!"

After Dad's Homegoing, the tax man and the accountant told me, "That man's records say more about his Christian commitment than anyone could ever put into words."

How happily he died. On my last visit, he again expressed his desire to be with the Lord. I prayed, "Lord, Thou hast promised that if we delight ourselves in Thee, Thou wilt give us the desires of our heart. Dad delighted himself in Thee. Now he wants to depart. He wants to go to Heaven. Give him his desire." Dad mustered full voice and said, "Amen." And that's the last word he said in this life.

Oh, he underwrote the training of six leaders. He leveraged his resources, and there are 600-plus missionaries out there because he leveraged time, relationships, prayer, information, and money.

Defined strategic effort made to achieve the optimum desired result.

Three ways to begin

First, recognize your responsibility.

Moreover it is required in stewards that a man be found faithful (1 Corinthians 4:2).

As you recognize your responsibility, ask God to

baptize you with a spirit of gratitude for His blessings. Remember what the Lord teaches in the parables. He requires you to leverage your resources. He never condemned a bad investment, only no investment. You'll never really prosper, believe me, until you obey the Lord in this matter.

In 1948, the press announced that the richest man in South Carolina had forty million dollars. But his stomach was so riddled with ulcers that he couldn't eat a piece of steak. I could eat the steak and couldn't afford it. Who was the wealthier?

Second, visualize the possibilities.

As you visualize, keep repeating God's promises. Scripture cannot lie. Visualize touching the world with your resources. If you own forty suits and you only wear six of them, you're paying storage for thirty-four suits. You no more possess them than if you had never bought them.

But the money could have transformed some lives in the world. If you're laden down with things that do not enrich your life, you have to ask yourself if those things are, in fact, impoverishing you.

Third, lay out your strategy.

Review your resources. You have time, relationships, influence, opportunity, money and, of course, prayer. Write it out. Develop daily the discipline of habitually moving forward in some way toward your God-honoring target. Enrich your life by making God's will your dream.

In November 1965, I took my IBM dictating unit to be repaired at the Finlayson Building in

Singapore. While there, I met the head of IBM for Southeast Asia, Mr. Mac Overton, well known to our own Pat Patterson who was mentored by him. In conversation, Overton asked me if I'd ever heard the name of John Sung. I said I had.

Almost fifty years earlier, John Sung had left the home of his preacher father in China. He clandestinely boarded the ship to America as a stowaway.

Immediately he set new scholastic records — all the way through to his Ph.D. at Ohio State.

He turned down plum positions with Standard Oil and the University of Minnesota. He returned to his native China. When he got to the South China Sea, he threw his Western clothes into the sea, and put on the blue denim robe of the China peasant.

He not only threw his old clothes into the water, but also all of his awards except his Ph.D. diploma.

When he arrived home, his father said, "John, now you can teach at the university and give your six brothers an education." In a way uncharacteristic of the Chinese, John Sung refused. He said, "Father, the Lord has called me to be an evangelist. He has told me I have only fifteen years to live."

And preach he did. He was twenty-nine at the time. He preached three times a day, six days a week, eleven months a year. The leverage of John Sung's ministry revolutionized the Chinese world.

Indonesian political leaders told me that 15,000 young men whom he had won to faith in Christ in 1938 and organized into five thousand teams, three to a team, played a crucial role in impeding the advance of Communism.

On the night of 30 September 1965, when the Communists attempted to subjugate Indonesia, God raised up a military man named Suharto to foil the plot.

Asian and Western experts have written that if Indonesia had been lost, Singapore, Malaysia, Thailand, Burma, Indochina, the Philippines and probably Australia, New Zealand, and the South Sea Islands would also have fallen.

Mac Overton said, "Did you know that the money IBM makes here in Southeast Asia contributes more to the bottom line than the money they are making in the U.S.?" He went on, "Had it not been for the preaching of John Sung, which created the climate, we would not have this kind of money."

So all of you who have IBM stock, Coca-Cola stock, American Express stock, Singer Sewing Machine stock, Caterpillar stock and all the rest, I want to tell you something. You would not only lack the freedom you enjoy today, but you would also lack the wealth you enjoy today, were it not for this one man whose name you probably never heard before because it has never appeared in the *New York Times.*

I'm not pressuring anybody. You're going to answer to the Lord one day. So the only pressure that you feel is the Holy Spirit leading you. You've had opportunity to see what God has done through some of these stellar leaders who have taken the advanced training provided by Haggai Institute. We do not train leaders for leadership's sake; we train them for evangelism's sake.

The First Presbyterian Church of Rome, Georgia, invited me there for a mission weekend. They said they had forty-six missionaries. I said, "Oh, no you don't. You've got over 846 because you've underwritten eight sponsorships. And each leader you've trained, on average, has trained more than a hundred more."

You'll notice I've used no tear-jerking stories. I'm a pretty hard-bitten realist. We do not resort to cheap, gaudy emotion or maudlin sentiment. Here are the facts as we know them. And to the best of my ability I try to pass them on.

I pray that every person reading this will say, "I do want to make a difference, and I here and now resolve, by God's grace, to take specific action to achieve the optimum desired result."

1
ASK BIGGER, THINK HIGHER

W hen I accepted the pastorate in Louisville, Kentucky, in 1954, I asked the Lord to prosper the ministry. He gave me a vision for the church that made no sense to the average believer.

Thank God, He gave me a group who caught the vision and acted on it. Within the first year, the Lord gave us unprecedented victories. If you did not get there early on a Sunday night, you had a difficult time finding a seat.

The prayer meeting attendance on Wednesday night grew enormously, from an average of 70 to several hundred, peaking at over 850.

Between 250 and 350 people showed up each Thursday night for visitation in the extended community.

Within the first 12 months, more people were added to the church by conversion and baptism than in any other church of the 11 leading denominations.

The missions giving increased by 600 percent, to a whopping 40 percent of the total budget.

During my first week in town, I went down to the corner of Fourth Street and Broadway and asked 24 people where the church was located.

Not one of them had heard of the church. Within a year, it was the most talked about church in the city, and always in the context of the truth it proclaimed.

I am not saying this to impress you. What happened in Louisville demonstrates and underscores an eternal principle. It is this: The God we serve continually calls us to overreach ourselves.

The overreaching principle

First, what could be more emphatic than our Lord's imperative command to evangelize?

This command dominated everything He said between His resurrection and ascension. Matthew, Mark, Luke, John, and Acts all emphasize the primacy of it. Matthew records Jesus saying, *"Make disciples in all nations."* Mark records Him saying, *"Preach the Gospel to every creature."* In Luke, *"Preach repentance and remission of sins to all nations, beginning at Jerusalem."* And in John, *"As the Father sent me, so I am sending you."*

Note — in passing — that the Lord commands not only the action but also the location: In all nations. To every creature. Looking at some churches, you might suppose Jesus had said, "Make disciples in your own back yard." He did not!

Second, what could be more emphatic than the sheer scale of the task involved?

Worldwide, more than 2.3 billion have no knowledge of Jesus Christ and His saving death and resurrection.

As a Christian, I am ashamed to tell you that more people know the name Coca-Cola than know the name Jesus Christ. Partial obedience is disobedience. Our Lord requires compliance with both parts of the Great Commission — making disciples in all nations.

But, how can that be when 72 percent of the non-Western population exists in countries that severely restrict or flatly prohibit Western missionaries? We are faced with an imperative summons and a seemingly impossible task.

Third, we are given an inexhaustible supply of God's power.

In John 14:12, Jesus says, *"He that believeth on me, the works that I do shall he do, and greater works than these shall he do, because I go to My Father."*

God calls us to overreach ourselves because His reach is so much longer than ours. As Paul wrote to the Ephesians:

> *Now to Him who is able to do exceedingly*
> *abundantly above all that we ask or think,*
> *according to the power that works in us*
> (Ephesians 3:20).

Dr. Han Kyung Chik, with a handful of refugees, built a larger church membership, a larger church budget, and founded more daughter churches than any other church in Christian history. He did it in just 17 years, in what was then the world's poorest nation.

That's *"exceedingly abundantly above all that we ask or think."*

John Wesley understood this, and put no limits on what God could do. He knew that *God puts no limits on faith, and faith puts no limits on God.*

His ministry resulted in:

- the first-ever prison reforms,
- the first-ever organized orphanage movement,
- the first-ever free hospital dispensary,
- the cessation of slave trading through convert William Wilberforce,
- the inspiration for Booth to found the Salvation Army, and J. Hudson Taylor to found the China Inland Mission.

That's *"exceedingly abundantly above all that we ask or think."*

When the Lord dropped in my lap the responsibility of starting this ministry, Haggai Institute, I objected in my spirit. Johnny, our son with cerebral palsy, needed me to be near home. Nonetheless, I had no alternative but to act on the Lord's directive.

I knew the concept was sound. I also suspected that many Christian leaders, good and godly, to be sure, would not even grasp it. No one in history — in business or religion — had raised funds for a secret program 10,000 miles away. We could not broadcast on radio, minister over television, or promote the ministry in publications.

Using the mass media — print or electronic — would put at risk the lives of our leaders serving, for instance, in the Islamic world.

The Muslim terrorists know exactly who we are and what we do. To billboard this ministry of love would incur their wrath.

The first session in 1969 gathered 19 leaders from four countries. By 2000, the total number trained had reached more than 38,500. That's an increase of more than 20,000 percent!

That's *"exceedingly abundantly above all that we ask or think."*

During that time the income rose from $240,000 annually to about $20,000,000 for this fiscal year — an 8,400 percent increase.

That's *"exceedingly abundantly above all that we ask or think."*

Today, over 65,500 leaders, trained at Haggai Institute, evangelize in 178 nations..

Before their acceptance, the leaders make a solemn commitment. They agree to endeavor to pass on the training to at least 100 peers within 24 months after their return from the training.

That's *"exceedingly abundantly above all that we ask or think."*

Our Haggai Institute donors have vision. Only Divine illumination could have enabled them to grasp it. It took greater vision for them than it did for me. I was on the scene. I visited the countries.

With my background, doors opened — doors not normally opened to Americans. Without this advantage, they were able to convert into reality concepts that the world scoffed at.

Consensus thinking never sidetracked them. They saw that something needed to be done, and so, undergirded by humility and an unswerving commitment to our Lord's command, they poured their energies and resources into the work of world evangelism.

And all the time, the donors faithfully tithed to their churches, indeed demonstrating the priority attention they gave to their churches.

That's *"exceedingly abundantly above all that we ask or think."*

Now what I've said about them, I can say about our worldwide staff. Recently they gave the money ($250,000) to underwrite an entire session. I'm moved by their vision, their generosity, and their industry.

> *Now to Him Who is able to do exceedingly*
> *abundantly above all that we ask or think*
> *according to the power that works in us . . .*
> *unto Him be glory in the church by Jesus*
> *Christ throughout all ages, world without end.*

Do you take the Scripture seriously?

Above what you ask or think

When you pray, do you believe that He is able? When you undertake an assignment, whether it be in business or home or church, do you, deep down in your soul, believe that He is able to see you through to victory? Or are you a timid "I hope so" believer?

What does the Word mean by saying "He is able to do above all that we ask?"

James writes, *"You have not because you ask not"* (James 4:2).

Why stumble when He is able to do what you ask?

I stuttered and stammered like an arc light in trouble until I was in my late teens. I went without meals to get enough money to sit under the famous Chicago speech coach, Professor J. Manley Phelps.

For years he coached the late Illinois United States Senator Everett Dirksen, arguably one of Washington's premier orators.

I nearly died of cholera at six months; of smallpox at six years; and of a rare sickness that prevented me from walking or talking until I was more than three years old.

At 16, I was brutalized in an accident.

The surgeon did not expect me to live. When I recovered, several doctors said I would not survive to 40. Both Prudential Life Insurance Company and National Life and Accident Insurance Company charged me a 25 percent penalty on my insurance premium every year because they said I would not live to be 40.

I looked to Him who is able to do what I asked — indeed, more than I asked.

Here I am, at 83. I have been told that I am the only person over 70 on medical records, from Harvard to Southwest Medical School, who does not have a speck of calcium in the heart.

He is able to do *exceedingly abundantly* more than I can ask.

In 1963, I reduced my income from $55,000 a year to $16,200 a year, plus $6,000 in expense moneys. I did not get a raise for 12 years. Johnny was costing us more than $10,500 a year. That does not equate, does it?

The Lord held us together, although things were very, very rough, though I did not breathe it to anybody, including family members.

We had no family financial legacy on either side. With an income below that of more than 34 ministers in the greater Atlanta area, by the grace of God, we are now able to give more in a year than I once expected to be my total life income.

He is able to do *more* than I asked.

When I was studying for the ministry, nobody wanted me to preach — or even teach a Sunday school lesson. They liked the way I played the trumpet.

So, they would assign me the music part of the service.

I knew the Lord had called me to preach; I didn't want to be a trumpet player the rest of my life. So I hocked my trumpet at the pawnshop. Since I could no longer play, they asked me to teach a class, and then later to preach.

Since no church would call me, I founded a church in Ainsworth, Indiana. That assured me of a place to preach every Sunday.

Today I have speaking assignments well into 2011, if the Lord does not return.

He is able to do *exceedingly abundantly above all* that I could ask or think.

Do we ask the Lord for a national awakening? If not, why not? John Knox said, "Give me Scotland or I die." It is said that Mary Queen of Scots feared John Knox more than all the armies of the earth!

Do you ask the Lord for wisdom in making money? Wisdom in managing money? Guidance in distributing money?

Do you call upon Him for guidance in every matter that worries or disturbs you?

What does the Word mean by saying "He is able to do above all that we can ask or think"?

The word "think" could be translated "comprehend" or "perceive."

As a ten-year-old boy, I committed my life to China. When I was ready, China was closed.

Shortly before her death, my mother returned to me a letter I wrote her when I was 21. I told of my plans to start a Bible institute in China. I planned to recruit my boyhood friend Dr. Gordon Eaton to found and head up a hospital. My plans also called for another classmate, Dick Reed, to establish a Christian radio station.

That never came about. But today, Haggai Institute deals with more Chinese people in one month — both in the People's Republic and in the overseas Chinese communities — than we could have reached in a lifetime with my initial plans.

More than I could comprehend or perceive.

God has blessed me with a great dream machine. I never turned it off. In fact, sometimes I think it is more active now than when I was a preteen.

And, I don't subjugate my dreams to memories; that's a sure route to failure.

I do not discuss the plans I have for my own life since I don't want my close friends to reserve me a suite in the funny farm.

In John 14:12, Jesus said that we are going to do more than He did. We had better get to it and determine how He wants us to go about it.

Is your imagination under Divine control or have you finally shut down your dream machine? Have you yielded to the taunts and the negative thinking of people around you who, themselves, have never accomplished much for God?

All great achievements begin with the imagination. Walt Disney called it "imagineering." He started out as a cartoonist with the *St. Louis Globe Democrat*. His imagination developed one of the great empires of the world. Why should people in the secular field be more imaginative and creative than those of us who are committed to the projection of the Gospel throughout the whole world?

How much time do you spend in actively bringing your imagination under the control of the Holy Spirit?

Casting down imaginations, and every high thing that exalteth itself against the knowledge of God, and bringing into captivity every thought to the obedience of Christ (2 Corinthians 10:5).

What precisely have you imagined in terms of your personal obedience to the command of the Lord concerning world evangelism? And what have been the results?

How many more people are hearing the Gospel today than heard it last year because of your sanctified imagination and commitment to the Lord's leadership?

Do you comprehend the possibility of generating more funds than you ever dreamed possible? And if so, to what end?

In 1971, a dear friend of mine said, "I have set my goal to make $10,000,000."

I looked him in the eye and said, "Why?"

He could not answer me. A passion to make money without a legitimate reason for its use will fail. The money may be acquired, but whether it's broken health, or broken relationships or jealousies — it will fail.

Paul the Apostle said to the Corinthians, the wealthiest people at that time, in 2 Corinthians 9:10 (paraphrased):

> *God gives seed to the farmers and provides everyone with food. He will increase what you have so that you can give even more to those in need. You will be blessed in every way, and you will be able to keep on being generous.*

He is able to do *above all* that we ask or think. Do you believe the Scriptures? It doesn't say here that the Lord will just give us what we ask or think. It says He will give us more. That should put the thrill of the Holy Ghost in every fiber of your being.

He says abundantly more! The word means "over and above." More than is necessary, super-added.

It also can mean "superior, extraordinary, surpassing, uncommon."

The Lord has spoken all day to 5,000. They are hungry. A lad gives Jesus five loaves and two fish. The Lord provides abundantly for every person, that is, to feed everyone to the full. No, He does more: He provides exceedingly abundantly — superabundantly. How do we know? They took up 12 baskets full of food more than the crowd could eat.

God asked Solomon what he wanted. Solomon asked for wisdom. The Lord gave him wisdom, but He also gave him power and riches and honor. He gave exceedingly abundantly, that is, exceeding what Solomon asked for. It was beyond measure of Solomon's expectation.

The Apostle Paul said that he was "*in labors more abundant*" (2 Corinthians 11:23). That is, he did more than was expected. He went farther, worked harder, put himself on the stretch.

But that's not all. He says: "*The Lord will do exceedingly abundantly or* [superabundantly] *above what we can ask or think*" Can you understand that? I cannot. I try, but my mind is drowned in the fathomless billows of our loving and giving God.

Therefore, we conclude that:

- God is able.
- He is able to do what we ask or think.
- He is able to do more than we ask or think.
- He is able to do abundantly more than we ask or think.
- He is able to do exceedingly abundantly more than we ask or think.

Now I will ask you candidly. Precisely what is it that you think, and to what end?

Remember that James said, *"You have not because you ask not"* (James 4:2). But then he went further, and said, *"And you ask things that you may consume them upon your own lusts, your own desires."*

What do you ask for that will honor God?

I hope some of you will be thinking of millions, even billions, and ask Him for such funds if they will be directed to world evangelism. Why? So you can and will reverse the drift away from global missions. So you will be the Holy Spirit's agent in reaching millions with the Gospel.

Wesley said, "Earn all you can, and save all you can, and give all you can, for as long as ever you can." And he did it. In today's terms he was a multimillionaire. He gave it all to the work of evangelism so that at his death his net worth was less than 40 pounds.

Moses was taking up an offering. He had to tell the Israelites to stop giving. They gave so much that he said they had more than they needed. Would not that be a blessing today? When did you last hear a Christian organization say, "Please — stop sending us funds!"? How many churches or institutions do you know that have all the money they can wisely use to carry out the will of God?

Instead, you hear people whining about the NASDAQ tanking more than any index in history. You hear people saying, with one breath, "I believe God," and with the next saying, "Do you realize this was the worst year financially since 1973-74 and maybe, for some people, worse than 1929?"

How can you move in the direction that your thought repels?

"Gird up the loins of your mind" (1 Peter 1:13), says the Apostle. Make sure your thoughts honor the Lord, and then ask Him, without timidity, for the things that He has put in your imagination — assuming that it is all for the glory of God.

Peter preached, and two entire cities turned to the Lord: Lydda and Saron. Superabundantly above all that Peter could have asked or thought.

The power inside you

What does the Word mean by *"according to the power that works in us"* (Ephesians 3:20)?

Just this: He supplies us with resurrection power! That gives me goose bumps.

It's the inexpressible and unlimited power that God used in creation. This same power — the power that put the sun and stars in place — works in us, drives us, energizes us.

Note that the Apostle says *"according to His power"* and not "out of His power." There is a crucial difference.

Suppose a beggar asked Dr. Bill Hinson to give him $2.00 for a sandwich. I can just hear our CEO saying, "Well, let me first see the sandwich!"

I can see Dr. Hinson pulling out his wallet bulging with hundred-dollar bills. So he takes his thumb and flips through the hundred-dollar bills until he finds two little curled-up one-dollar bills. He gives those bills to the beggar.

Now, he would be giving out of his ability, but not according to his ability!

God does not give out of His power; He gives according to His power.

Now if that doesn't put your soul on shouting ground, I don't know what will. As the great African-American preacher, Dr. S. M. Lockridge, would say, "If that doesn't light your fire, your wick is wet. If that doesn't ring your bell, your clapper is busted."

You limit your available resources when you maintain an "out of" instead of "according to" mind-set.

You can never ask too much. You can never think too broadly, too grandly. All you must do is ensure that the thinking, the asking, and the imagining focus on glorifying God.

This is how God gives according to His power in world evangelism.

One, God gives according to His power in vision.

You are praying in vain if you can't see it — unless you pray, "Lord, work in my mind that my thoughts will be Your thoughts. Enlighten me. Let me visualize the carrying out of Your command. Help me to grasp that anything You command is possible."

Two, God gives according to His power in prayer for world evangelism.

The disciples met in the upper room and continued with one accord in prayer. The Scripture commands us to pray — urging prayers and supplications with giving of thanks for all men, including heads of state.

How many of us could name as many as ten heads of state outside the Western group of nations? How then can we pray for people we don't even know exist? It takes skull work.

Our monthly prayer calendar will help you here if you just ask for it. Prayer is tough — but it yields glorious and eternal results.

Three, God gives according to His power in money for world evangelism.

When I was 38 years old, Robert Woodruff, the majordomo of Coca-Cola, invited me to lunch with him in his private dining room. He said, "Young preacher, it doesn't take any brains to make money. If you work hard and treat people well, you can make money. It takes a few brains to manage money. Not a lot, but a few brains to manage money."

Then he leaned forward in his chair. "But I tell you, it takes nothing less than God-given genius to give it away intelligently."

I have never forgotten that.

Repeatedly, I am asked, "How much money do you need?" I reply, "That's not the question. The question is, 'What does the Lord require of you?'"

When you stand before God, it won't do for you to say, "Lord, I understand Haggai Institute did very well; they prepared thousands of leaders for evangelism." The Lord will say, "But how many who never heard the Gospel could have heard the Gospel if you had added to the income and made possible the outreach that I intended?"

Study the history of this ministry, and you will know that the Lord has done exceedingly abundantly above all we could ask or think.

The trustees pay all of the overhead, all of the expenses. Every dollar you give goes directly to the training.

Frequently I have asked our veteran donors: Have your gifts achieved what you expected? One man told me, "Exceedingly, abundantly above all I could ask or think." He knew that was one of my favorite texts.

Paul J. Meyer said, "I don't give because I like Haggai Institute, though I do. I don't give because I like John Haggai, though I do. I give because I think Haggai Institute gives me the biggest bang for the buck in world evangelism."

An Indonesian pastor came to the training in 1978. He started his ministry with only six members, in Surabaya, Indonesia's second largest city, a metropolitan area of seven million. The church he dedicated recently seats 20,000 people. Next to the church, he has a multiple-story leadership center where he continues to train people. All it cost the Haggai Institute donor was one sponsorship. How do you like that for return on the money?

Two donors visited the church of an accomplished alumnus in Rio de Janeiro — Dr. Miguel Angelo. One donor asked, "How do we explain to people back home what we have just seen?"

I said, "You don't."

God seems to have given some people the ability to comprehend what they have not personally experienced.

I pray for each donor of Haggai Institute. I pray that their churches may prosper. And I pray that they may prosper. And, I can tell you, they have.

Any farmer, over the course of years, will have a drought, a flood, or pestilence. But, to the degree that he is faithful in observing the laws of agriculture and agronomy, he will prosper.

I think the Lord lets us have these dips to remind us that He is able; we are not. He is able to do; we are not. He is able to do what we ask or think; we are not. He is able to do superabundantly more than we can ask or think.

What a thought!

Are you ready to ask bigger and think higher, so that you can cash in on our Lord's ability and desire to fulfill in your life — *exceedingly abundantly above all that* [you] *can ask or think?*

8
IT'S ALL BEEN DONE BEFORE

Here are some statistics from the recently published *World Christian Encyclopedia.*

During the first year of this millennium, global Christianity spent $270 billion in U.S. dollars on the various activities of the church.

Of that amount, $255 billion in U.S. dollars were spent within the borders of the country of the donor.

That means only $15 billion — 5.5 percent of the total — went to "foreign missions."

And only $54 million was spent in outreach to the more than 1.6 billion people who have never once heard the Gospel. Just $54 million spent in outreach to 1.6 billion unevangelized.

What does that mean? Here's what it boils down to. If you had never heard the Gospel in the year 2000, the total resources spent on reaching you by the worldwide church that year was 3.4 cents.

I wonder what the Apostle Paul would have made of that. More than any other person mentioned in Acts, Paul demonstrated in his life the way in which we should be going about world evangelism. He "modeled missions" for us.

Read carefully the Word of the Lord, from Romans 15:19b-24 (NIV):

So from Jerusalem all the way around to Illyricum, I have fully proclaimed the gospel of Christ. It has always been my ambition to preach the gospel where Christ was not known, so that I would not be building on someone else's foundation. Rather, as it is written: "Those who were not told about him will see, and those who have not heard will understand." This is why I have often been hindered from coming to you. But now that there is no more place for me to work in these regions, and since I have been longing for many years to see you, I plan to do so when I go to Spain. I hope to visit you while passing through and to have you assist me on my journey there, after I have enjoyed your company for a while.

Paul modeled motivation

Have you seen the Olympics?

Paul may have watched the summer Olympics 2,000 years ago in his boyhood hometown of Tarsus in Turkey. These athletic events, as you know, go back to ancient Greece. The apostle was familiar — very familiar — with athletic contests. He mentions some of the games in his letters to the churches.

He talks about racing — that refers to the chariot race. He talks about wrestling. He talks about boxing. "I don't do shadow boxing," he says (see 1 Corinthians 9:26). He talks about running the race with patience (Hebrews 12:1). In fact, he reveled in using a foot race as an illustration of our effort in the Christian life.

Now he writes in this passage about his ambition. The King James translates it, *"I have strived"* (Romans 15:20). In Paul's day, as in ours, runners extended their chest to break the tape. And this is what Paul is saying, "I am pressing forward. I am straining at every point to reach the tape first."

To the Philippians (3:13-14), he talks about pressing on. He says, *"This one thing I do."* Too many Christians today live a life that shouts, "These 50 things I dabble in."

Paul modeled the message

Unfortunately, the translators of the New Testament had the same aversion to the word "evangelism" that we find endemic in Christian circles today.

The verb *euangelizo* and the noun, *euangelion* appear 132 times in the New Testament. When Paul says here, "I have fully proclaimed the Gospel of Christ," and again where he says, "It has always been my ambition to preach the Gospel," in both cases the word is "evangelize." "I have fully evangelized." And, "It is my aim to evangelize."

When we read in Romans 1:16, *"I am not ashamed of the Gospel,"* the better translation is "I am not ashamed of evangelism."

In verse 15, when he says *"I am ready to preach the Gospel to you that are in Rome,"* he is saying, "I am ready to evangelize in Rome."

You will notice that we emphasize the term "world evangelism." That is our emphasis. We believe in missions. Missions simply means the act or the process of sending. Thanks to people like you, more than 65,500 have been sent to 178 nations of the world. These "sent ones" evangelize.

Paul would have liked that. He modeled the message, and we have adopted his model.

Paul's formula

Paul insisted upon self-propagation, self-government, and self-support.

He did not import money, except in the one case of taking the money from Greece to Jerusalem.

He did not import personnel.

He did not import program format.

He broke open the ground and let the Holy Spirit do His work through local believers.

He was in Thessalonica only three Sabbaths. That could have been a minimum of two weeks or a maximum of four weeks. And yet he was able to say shortly thereafter, *"From you has sounded forth the Word of the Lord . . . in every place your faith to God-ward is spread abroad; so that we need not to speak anything"* (1 Thessalonians 1:8).

Sometime I will deliver a major message on evangelism and discipleship. Suffice it to say now, that there is no such thing as Biblical discipleship that does not major in developing people along the lines of evangelism — getting them to evangelize. Evangelism is bringing people to Christ. Discipleship is designed to multiply converts.

Paul modeled the methods

First, Paul stayed tuned to the Holy Spirit.
For example, he wanted to go to Bithynia. The Holy Spirit told him to go to Troas. If he had not followed the Holy Spirit's vision:

- He never would have received the Macedonian vision.
- The Gospel would not have made it into Europe.
- Lydia and those with her never would have come to know Christ.
- The Philippian jailer and his family would never have entered into peace with God.

Paul said the Holy Spirit had ordered him to visit Jerusalem. Disciples in Tyre, who met with him on his way to Jerusalem, told him not to go.

Then, in Caesarea, the godly Agabus and some others warned Paul against going to Jerusalem. Paul was undeterred. He proceeded to Jerusalem.

Though he loved and respected those who advised him against it, he had to follow the leading of the Holy Spirit.

In exactly the same way, he followed the leading of the Holy Spirit when he determined to go *"not where Christ was named"* (Romans 15:20).

That took courage. That took total reliance on God. That took a strength of character inexplicable except in terms of divine empowerment.

Paul stayed tuned to the Holy Spirit. A priority for Paul is a priority for Haggai Institute — to go *"not where Christ is named."*

Second, Paul strategized creatively.

When God gave him an idea, he didn't call for a focus group to check it over. He ran with it. Whether the people stuck with him or fell away, he pushed on.

God's ideas are always strategic, creative, and effective. Has he not given us the blueprint in the book of Acts?

Paul's strategic plans focused on geography — to go *"not where Christ was named."*

They focused on religious demographics — to go *"not where Christ was named."*

They focused on cultural demographics — to go *"not where Christ was named."*

The Apostle Paul did not want to build on another person's foundation. He refused to deviate from his commitment to go where Christ was not named.

He based his strategy on logic. Why should anyone hear the Gospel twice before everyone has heard the Gospel once?

And why should he put himself in competition with other Christian leaders? Paul understood the poisonous effect of envy. By going where Christ was not named, he would not elicit the kind of envy that he encountered in Greece and in Jerusalem.

Paul's tolerance was immense.

In Philippians he said he rejoiced that even those who preach Christ out of envy and strife at least are preaching the Gospel. Nevertheless, logic counseled that he put himself outside the parameters of the envy circle.

I repeat, in his strategy, Paul thought creatively.

Consensus thinking is never creative thinking. In the establishment of any enterprise, consensus thinking rarely achieves spectacular results.

Gutenberg was not a consensus thinker. He developed the printing press. What a debt we owe him. He may have been the greatest contributor to the development of the Western World.

Wernher von Braun, the mastermind behind the American space program, was not a consensus thinker. Henry Ford was not a consensus thinker.

Dr. Cho of Korea, the builder of the largest church in Christian history, did not fall prey to consensus thinking.

As soon as Cho's effectiveness surfaced, during the late 1970s and early 1980s, a never-ending stream of American Christian leaders made a pilgrimage to see how it was done.

When they returned and implemented his program, it didn't work as effectively as they had expected. Cho knew his people, his culture, and his nation; and he, under the leadership of the Holy Spirit, created a program that has had no equal in two thousand years.

It was part of Paul's method to strategize creatively. And a priority for Paul is a priority for Haggai Institute — to go not where Christ is named.

Third, Paul focused on leaders and new territories.

His missionary journeys clearly underscore his strategy of meeting with leaders. Indeed, Christian history, as we have it from the church fathers and Eusebius, verifies his focus on leaders as well as new territories.

Who could have read his letters to the churches? Only the literate. And who constituted the literate? The wealthy and influential — in other words, the leaders. Only 3–5 percent of the people of the Middle East were literate at that time. So, the church heard Paul's messages through the mediation of the leaders, the literati.

Too often I hear the statement, "The poor people heard Christ gladly." While many of the poor people did hear Christ gladly, the Bible never makes any such statement.

The Scriptures say the common people heard Christ gladly. The word common comes from the Greek word, *polus*. The word is never translated poor people but common people.

It refers to quantity. It is translated "many," "numerous," "great," "abundant," "plenteous." That word can include people like erudite Nicodemus and wealthy Joseph of Arimathea just as accurately as it can include the blind beggar, Bartimaeus.

Tell me any enterprise that was ever begun by anyone other than the leader.

Many of you reading this are business people. Did you start your business with the shipping clerk? You may have done the work of the shipping clerk, but you started with the CEO (yourself) and you hired under you, not over you. Is that not true?

Pastors reading this have established churches. Did you establish the church with the janitor? You may have done the work of the janitor, but you brought in staff under you, not over you.

Some of you are educators. Have you ever heard of a school that was started by a custodian? The headmaster or the principal may have done the work of the custodian, but he hired people under him, not over him.

Rarely have I heard of anybody, read of anybody, or met anybody who came to Christ through the influence of one who was at a much lower socioeconomic or intellectual level.

True, there are some. For instance Maria Millis, the servant girl, won Anthony Ashley Cooper (Lord Shaftesbury) to faith in Christ. However, it was the Moravians who won John Wesley, Edward Kimball who won Dwight L. Moody, Dwight L. Moody who won Sir Wilfred Grenfell, Mordecai Ham who won teenage Billy Graham.

Paul's passion to go to Spain underlines this strategy of going to new areas and of meeting with leaders.

Spain was the westernmost nation of the then-civilized world. One may say it was the limit of the civilized world. That very fact would lure Paul to preach there. His passion focused on going where Christ was not named.

Spain was a center of leadership, erudition, and achievement. Lucan, the epic poet; Martial, the master of epigram; Quintilian, the greatest teacher of oratory in his day — all were Spaniards.

Even more, Seneca, the great stoic philosopher who became the prime minister under Emperor Nero, was a Spaniard.

The English scholar, Bishop J.B. Lightfoot, reminds us that Seneca was a contemporary of Paul the Apostle. Born probably within a few years of each other, the Christian apostle and the stoic philosopher both lived in Rome, both died about the same time, and both fell victim to the same tyrant's rage.

Paul may have thought, "If only I could reach the spiritual darkness of Spain with the light of the Gospel, tremendous victories could ripple throughout the world."

Paul was the consummate strategist.

Haggai Institute has modeled its program after his methods. We focus on leaders. We focus our most intense efforts on areas where Christ is not named.

In Paul's day, it was the West where Christ had not been named. In our day, it's the East.

Those who do not know intimately the demographic makeup of Haggai Institute alumni do not realize that the people we train qualify as distinguished leaders.

Haggai Institute does not train them to lead; they know that already. We give them "advanced leadership training," with an emphasis upon the "how" of evangelism within their respective cultures. These folks know the "why," and they yearn to know the "how." The goal is that they may be effective in presenting Jesus Christ without compromise and without offense.

They are doing the work *"not where Christ was named."*

They include media personalities; jurists, from lawyers to high court justices; university presidents; multinational businessmen; three vice presidents of nations; clergy, from evangelists to archbishops; medical people, from hospital administrators to head surgeons, including every area of medicine from cardiology to radiology; authors; urban planners; architects — the list goes on and on.

Paul focused on leaders and closed territories. A priority for Paul is a priority for Haggai Institute — to go *"not where Christ was named."*

Fourth, Paul maintained a nonstop relationship with his people.

He was an indefatigable traveler. And when he couldn't travel to meet his churches, he wrote letters to them. Paul worked tirelessly at keeping in contact.

In September 2006, I made my ninety-ninth trip around the world and visited China for the forty-second time. I don't do this because I like to travel. I would much prefer staying home. I travel to stay in touch with people.

The impact of personal contacts cannot be replaced with videotapes, cyberspace, movies or any other kind of intermediate communication.

Paul maintained a nonstop relationship with his people. A priority for Paul is a priority for Haggai Institute — to go *"not where Christ was named."*

Paul modeled the mind of Christ

Once committed to the Lord Jesus Christ, the apostle Paul changed the world with the weapons of love and prayer and witness.

As far as we know, he never got to Spain. Nero imprisoned him. For two years he languished in the dungeon. Finally he was executed.

It was the habit of the executioner in those days to recite the crimes for which the victim was about to be beheaded. I can hear the executioner asking Paul, "What is this God you worship doing for you now?"

Paul says, "I am not ashamed, for I know Whom I have believed and am persuaded that He is able to be my safety deposit vault against that day. I have fought the fight. I have kept the faith. I have finished the course. Henceforth, there is a crown of righteousness reserved for me, which I shall happily cast at my Savior's feet."

Paul was one of those rare individuals who fulfilled his commitment after the environment in which it was initially made had dissipated.

He understood the power of the permanent. He was not addicted to the "Project of the Month" mentality.

He believed we will all stand before the Judgment Seat of Christ. There we will give an answer for every idle word, for every idle deed — not just bad words and not just bad deeds — for every dollar misspent, for every hour squandered, for every influence not exploited for the glory of Christ, and for every opportunity not seized.

He was not ashamed of evangelism.

And again, may that be the passion in our hearts which melts the lead in our feet and the ice on our tongues, driving us to full obedience.

Paul modeled the money-support method

Paul says, "I hope to visit you while passing through and to have you assist me on my journey there, after I have enjoyed your company for a while."

The words translated "assist me" come from the Greek word *propempo*. In other places it is translated "accompany" or "attend" or "escort." In Titus 3:13-14, (NIV), Paul says:

> *Do everything you can to help Zenas the lawyer and Apollos on their way and see that they have everything they need.*

Our people must learn to devote themselves to

doing what is good, in order that they may provide for daily necessities and not live unproductive lives.

John the Apostle, in his third epistle, says to his friend Gaius:

> *They have told the church about your love.*
> *You will do well to send them on their way in*
> *a manner worthy of God* (3 John 1:6, NIV).

One hardly hears this discussed in Bible studies or in sermons. Paul makes a great deal of this "ministry of giving." He refers more specifically to it in describing to the Corinthians what the Macedonians did. Read 2 Corinthians 8:2-4, 8 (NIV). Here Paul boldly challenged Christians to give money to world evangelism. He told them about the Philippians who had given out of their poverty unto the riches of their liberality. He said:

> *Out of the most severe trial, their*
> *overflowing joy and their extreme poverty*
> *welled up in rich generosity. For I testify*
> *that they gave as much as they were able*
> *and even beyond their ability. Entirely on*
> *their own, they urgently pleaded with us for*
> *the privilege of sharing in this service to the*
> *saints . . . . I am not commanding you, but*
> *I want to test the sincerity of your love by*
> *comparing it with the earnestness of others.*

Now Paul says to the wealthy Corinthians, doubtlessly the wealthiest church at that time, "I don't mean that other men be eased and that the burden comes on you." In effect, what he is saying is that "the Philippians gave out of their need. I'm simply asking you to give out of your surplus."

Paul's approach is as relevant today as it was in the first century. That's why Haggai Institute patterns our world evangelism activities after it.

9
JUST DO THE MATH

In late August 1968, Donald Childs, a Green Beret, assumed his assigned position at Camp A-239, also called Duc Lap. This crucial American outpost was located only three miles from the Cambodian border.

Childs and two other Green Berets of the 403rd Special Forces Detachment faithfully fulfilled their duty at Camp A-239. Twelve men from another special forces group, a small company of Vietnamese commandos, and 350 lightly armed villagers stood alongside the three Green Berets.

In just five days, Donald Childs would complete his tour. Before the week was out, he would leave Vietnam forever. He'd come through the battles unscathed. He was looking forward to getting home to his family and loved ones.

That night, the Vietcong decided to take the Duc Lap camp.

They opened up on the camp with a barrage of heavy mortar, rocket, and small arms. The three men of the 403rd Special Operations Detachment manned their defensive positions. All night they returned fire with their 81mm mortar. They fired until the barrel overheated, then they cooled it with cold water and fired again.

Donald Childs did what he knew he had to do. He began to guide the women and children into the safety of the bunkers, telling the village men to remain on the perimeter defense.

For the next three days and two nights, the defenders of Duc Lap faced incessant fire and repeated waves of assaults.

The Duc Lap camp occupied positions on two small hills. Gradually the enemy gained control of the north hill and most of the saddle in between. The villagers drifted from their defensive positions, leaving the Vietcong within 50 yards of the American operations bunker.

Childs now faced a grim choice. He could stay where he was, and hope that reinforcements arrived in time. It's always easier to keep your head down and stay still! Or he could take the fight to the enemy.

He decided to assault the enemy.

He rallied the village men back to the perimeter for protection against enemy fire. Then he picked a 10-man force and led it into the enemy-held north hill. It was a hair-raising expedition.

Childs himself, in the company of a single Vietnamese medic, took on the job of cleaning out the enemy bunkers with grenades. At one point, an assault on the perimeter removed the protective fire, leaving Childs to single-handedly take on an entire squad of Vietcong.

When they finally scrambled back to the south hill, Childs noticed some B-40 rockets and rocket launchers lying abandoned downslope. He and the medic went back down to destroy them. In all,

Childs made three sorties down that sniper-ridden descent. When the medic got hit, Childs shook off his equipment and went back to get him, armed only with a pistol.

The action saved the camp.

Courageous? Without a doubt!

Rational? Well, that's a question worth pondering. What exactly would make you run into the open where 800 enemy troops can get a clean shot at you? What can make you disable those mental alarms that are built in to prevent your taking ill-advised, even suicidal action?

Here's the answer.

When God puts you in a tough situation — and make no mistake, when you're a believer there's no such thing as blind chance or bad luck — it's so you can grasp the initiative and reap the dividends of obedience.

Thank God, not many of us today face the kind of horror those Green Berets faced. But the principle is the same. In every tough situation, you have an option to obey. You may not find obedience easy or convenient. It may flout all our assumptions about what is prudent or reasonable. But we know it's the way forward — because God calls us to claim the obedience dividend.

Look at Abraham.

Now it came to pass after these things that God tested Abraham, and said to him, "Abraham!" And he said, "Here I am." Then He said, "Take now your son, your only son

Isaac, whom you love, and go to the land
of Moriah, and offer him there as a burnt
offering on one of the mountains of which I
shall tell you" (Genesis 22:1-2).

No person has any right to any opinion on any question where God has spoken.

God tested Abraham

That's God's pattern.

Abraham didn't expect it. Life was good. King Abimelech courted him. He had secured his wells. He was gladdened with the birth and maturity of Isaac. And he was friend to the everlasting God. Surely he must have thought, "I am now in Beulah-land. My remaining years are an unbroken chain of blessing."

As a bolt out of the sky came the summons of God.

And it touched Abraham at his most tender point. It concerned Isaac. Nothing else in the circumference of his life could have been such a test as this — focusing on the heir of promise, the child of his old age, the laughter of his life. God tested Abraham's love.

We don't like testing, but without it we don't mature. James said, *"Count it all joy when you fall into various testing"* (James 1:2). And Paul assures us that every test through which we pass is *"common to man,"* and God will not allow us to be tested above our ability to bear; He will make a way to endure through the test itself (see 1 Corinthians 10:13).

We fight the very means God uses to make us strong. Jesus Himself was subjected to this testing. *"Though He were a son yet learned He obedience through the things that He suffered"* (Hebrews 5:8).

Sometimes the test seems to make no sense.

God had promised, *"I will make of you a great nation, and your name shall be great. In you shall all the families of the earth be blessed"* (Genesis 12:2,3b). How then could God ask Abraham to sacrifice his only son — the son through whom those promises were to be fulfilled? It defied logic.

Was Abraham gambling that God would back down?

No — Abraham had received sealed orders in his younger years. At that time, God had told Abraham to leave his home comforts and move out of Ur of the Chaldeans. No destination. He just said *"to a land that I will show thee"* (Genesis 12:1).

And now, when God told him to sacrifice his only son, Abraham trusted God to reconcile an irrevocable promise with an apparently irrational command. Abraham didn't question God. He didn't argue. He obeyed.

Bob Pierce, the founder of World Vision, used to say, "Go as far as you can in the direction that God is leading. When you face a wall and there seems to be no possibility of pressing on, count upon God to make an opening in the wall."

As you must know, I believe in long-range, strategic planning. However, the planning process must never paralyze one's response to a definite directive that God gives — even when the directive comes in the form of sealed orders and leaves the end of the matter still in question.

But while God tested Abraham, He also trusted him.

He said in Genesis 18:19, *"For I have known Abraham, in order that he may command his children and his household after him, that they keep the way of the Lord."*

God trusts you, because of the indwelling Holy Spirit within you. He knows in your own strength you would fail and fall, but *"He Who hath begun a good work in you will perform it until the day of Jesus Christ"* (Philippians 1:6).

In every test, God makes *"a way of escape that you may be able to bear it"* (1 Corinthians 10:13). A test is not a tripwire, a booby trap to snare us. It is God's vote of confidence — a chance to show what He has done in us.

Years ago, New York State constructed a railroad bridge across the Hudson River. After its completion, one evening at dinner time, the residents on both sides of the Hudson heard the whistles of two trains. They rushed to the back porches to see the two trains with freight cars that took up every inch of the bridge.

Why did the engineers stop and blow the whistles? Why did they get out, shake hands, and laugh? To break down the bridge? Or to show how strong the bridge was? They did it to convince the neighboring residents they need not fear. The bridge was worthy.

God does not test you to break you down. He does it to prove your worth. To prove His presence in your life. And His sufficiency for all your needs.

The core issue is obedience

So Abraham rose early in the morning and saddled his donkey, and took two of his young men with him, and Isaac his son; and he split the wood for the burnt offering, and arose and went to the place of which God had told him (Genesis 22:3).

Apparently the command of God to offer up Isaac came to Abraham during the night. For early the next morning, he was on his way.

He could have said, "Perhaps I didn't understand the Lord."

He could have said, "I want to discuss this with some of my mentors. I want to pray about this with some of my brothers and sisters in Christ."

He obeyed. No questions. No argument. Full obedience.

Sometimes it's wrong to take time to pray. In Exodus 14:15, Moses was praying about the crisis in getting the Hebrews across the sea. God said, *"Wherefore criest thou unto Me? Speak unto the children of Israel that they go forward."* He was saying, "This is not the time to pray, Moses. This is the time to obey. Get moving."

You don't pray about whether or not you should obey the Great Commission. You don't pray whether or not you should tithe and give offerings. You don't pray about whether or not you should make world evangelism a priority. God has already commanded. Your only response is to obey.

First, Abraham obeyed God instantly.

Abraham did not procrastinate.

He had walked with God long enough to acquire the habit of immediacy. He "rose up early in the morning."

Every year I can enter in my diary the names of people who wrench their schedules to forward the cause of world evangelism.

There are some who, by faith, have committed unprecedented amounts of money, and they have fulfilled their commitment. They did this in order to undergird world evangelism through Haggai Institute. These deliberate and prudent people are in full control of their faculties at all times.

When they received the orders from God, they obeyed without delay. In some instances, they didn't know where the money was coming from.

Had Cecil Day delayed action on the command God gave him, there would have been no training center in Singapore. When he gave that half million dollars, he was in the throes of the oil embargo crisis with his entire empire facing collapse.

Had Carl and Janie Newton delayed for even four hours sending their $100,000 gift in September 1969, there would be no training program today. That was the largest single gift they had ever made. They didn't have available funds. God directed them to borrow the money. They did. And God prospered them.

My father was a cautious man. God moved him at the annual meeting in 1987 to underwrite an entire sponsorship of $9,100. When I saw his goal card, I was so sick, I felt like vomiting. I knew he didn't have that kind of money. Dad's salary never reached $20,000 a year.

Within a week, he had sent a check for the first thousand dollars. Before the end of the year, he completed his commitment without decreasing his gifts to other ministries.

Second, Abraham obeyed God completely.

He carried out the orders in every detail. He didn't say, "Well, I don't think it matters where I make the offering just as long as I make the offering. After all, one mountain is as good as another."

He didn't say, "God looks on the heart, and I'm sure He doesn't mean for me to take this command literally. Surely He doesn't mean for me to offer a burnt sacrifice of my son. He wants me to yield my son Isaac to Him for full-time Christian work or to use Isaac as He will."

At Haggai Institute, God commanded us to take the Gospel to those who otherwise would not hear. That includes the more than 2.5 billion in China and India. That includes the more than one billion in the Islamic world. Haggai Institute graduates currently work in every major Islamic nation.

Incomplete obedience to God's command is disobedience. Careless obedience is dead obedience; the heart is gone out of it.

Third, Abraham obeyed God confidently.

Abraham told the two young men, *"Abide here. The lad and I will go up yonder and worship and come again unto you."*

In his heart, he knew that God had some way of deliverance. He could not forecast what that deliverance would be. In Hebrews, we read he thought God would raise Isaac from the dead. Abraham, man of faith, knew that God could not lie. He believed God that in Isaac would his seed be multiplied and all the nations of the earth be blessed. He had an unwavering faith.

There's a message here for us. Are we willing to slay our brightest hopes, if God so commands, because we are so sure that He will not fail us or deceive us?

Trust God even though He asks you to do something that seems to doom your best interests. If you dare to do it, you will not only obtain the promise, but He shall also grant you some crowning and unexpected mark of His love.

Fourth, Abraham obeyed God directly.

Abraham could have delegated the job.

He could have said, "I'm 118 years old, I'm enjoying my golf game. If there's some unpleasant work to do, I'll send some of the young folk and let them look after it."

Delegation's a good thing. As my dear old friend the late Eddie Lieberman said, "If you don't delegate, you don't have an organization."

Abraham had an organization. He had at least 316 servants working for him. But he didn't delegate his obedience to God.

It's what you do today that matters

You cannot obey God yesterday. And you have no assurance you can obey God tomorrow. Your next breath is in God's hand.

Therefore, the question is: what will be your response today?

What if you knew that you would not see another sunrise? Would life be any different for you? Would things that didn't matter begin to matter? Would priorities change within the next few hours?

Abraham Maslow, the psychologist, had a near fatal heart attack. He recovered from that heart attack, but it literally changed his life in the process. His life from that point on, he called his "postmortem life." Everything was doubly precious, he said. You get stabbed by the very thought of being, of talking, of eating, of having friends. You see, what this psychologist discovered in his postmortem life was that happiness is hidden in the ordinary — in the day-by-day living.

Paul the Apostle could say to the Philippians, "You have progressed in your faith on a daily basis, from the first day until now. Day to day, you have trusted God. Day to day, you have depended on God for your needs."

You make your commitments today, trusting God to do what you cannot do tomorrow if, indeed, He gives you a tomorrow.

God's grace, God's mercy, God's provisions

come to us day by day as we need them. You can count on it.

God provided manna to the Israelities — enough supply for one day only. If they took more than one day's supply, it was filled with maggots. They couldn't eat it.

You remember the story of the widow of Zarephath? Elijah said, "I want you to fix me a meal. I'm hungry." She objected, saying she had only one meal left for her son and herself, and then they would die because there was no more food.

Elijah said, "You fix me the meal, and when you go back there will be oil. Every time you go back, there will be enough oil for the next meal. Every time you go back to the sack for the flour, there will be enough in the sack for the next meal."

In effect, Elijah was saying, "Make God a cake, first."

Here God was teaching her to trust Him one day at a time. But she had to make the commitment right then and there. If she had delayed, there would have been nothing but death for her son and herself.

Claim the Obedience Dividend

Around the end of the Cold War, a new phrase started appearing in the press. The phrase was "Peace Dividend."

It referred to the financial benefits of peace. All the resources formerly poured into defense and security spending to fend off the Soviet Bloc would now be available for social and domestic purposes. Schools, hospitals, housing, roads, etc. The spears of war could be beaten back into pruning hooks and used for peaceful purposes.

Looking back now, it's hard to see much evidence of the Peace Dividend. The spending diverted from military uses hasn't led to any noticeable improvement in social causes. And the Soviet Bloc has been replaced by new enemies requiring new and even deeper defense expenditure. There seems to have been little dividend from peace.

But there is a massive dividend to obedience. For Abraham — and for you.

God spared Isaac and provided the sacrifice required. With Isaac delivered, the promise was intact. The seed would be as the stars of heaven and as the sand upon the seashore. From that seed came the blessing for the whole world, our own Redeemer, the Lord Jesus Christ. And in that seed have all the nations of the earth been blessed.

In doing what God required, even against instinct, even against reason, Abraham claimed the Obedience Dividend.

I know you trust God, and I know it is your purpose to obey Him. The fact that you have carved out time to read this book strongly suggests you are a person of faith and obedience.

What you do in the next few minutes will have world-changing impact — because, like Abraham, you can claim the Obedience Dividend.

To do the work God wants us to do will require a minimum of $30 million over the coming year (2007).

That's more than we've ever raised. While perhaps none of us can do this alone, all of us together can do it.

A sponsorship costs $9,100. When you make a commitment to a sponsorship, you know that the person whom you sponsor has committed himself or herself, in writing, to endeavor to pass on the training to at least 100 others in his or her country within 24 months of returning home. Multiply by 10.

That's a one-time, only-time cost. Do you know what it would cost to support 1,000 missionaries? At least $60 million a year, every year, including the years they are home on furlough.

The cost for underwriting 100,000 American missionaries would be $6 billion. That's four times as much as all churches of all denominations in the U.S.A. and Canada give annually to evangelism in the non-West, nonwhite nations of the world!

One thousand Haggai Institute graduates will train over 100,000 in a two-year period.

That's the Obedience Dividend.

God bless the missionaries. May their number increase. When Dr. Rebecca Naylor finally had to return to the U.S.A., this last American missionary to India brought an end to traditional American missions to India.

Here is where Haggai Institute takes up the slack. India now has 4,800 H.I.-trained leaders in evangelism working in each of the Indian states, as well as across the subcontinent and many of the Arabian nations! And they are underwriting the costs in India!

But we haven't yet scratched the surface. Some of our donors can give many sponsorships. Some others can underwrite an entire session, roughly a quarter of a million dollars ($250,000.00). Several donors have underwritten multiple sessions, as high as four to eight sessions over the course of a year. On the other hand, some may strain to give a sponsorship of $9,100. It's according to what a man has, not what he doesn't have.

Abraham did not make his decision on the basis of what others were doing. He obeyed God's orders for him. You must do what God commands you to do. The response of others has no part in your decision. Your response is not to an appeal that I make. Your obedience is to GOD. It's to the appeal He makes to your own heart.

He may be challenging you to make a commitment of money greater than seems possible. Make that commitment. Some years ago, Guy Rutland went to his financial advisor and said, "I've made a commitment for $100,000. Now tell me how I can get it."

He was claiming the Obedience Dividend.

Don't let the devil paralyze your thinking by focusing on the "if only's."

- If only I had given money when I had it.
- If only I had not made such a bad business investment.
- If only I were not crippled by the horrendous costs of putting my children through the university.

- If only I could lay my hands on some big money.
- If only I didn't have so many other commitments.
- If only my family were more sympathetic to world evangelism.
- If only my children didn't resent my gifts to God's work.
- If only my children shared my priorities.
- If only I could liquidate some of my sorry assets.

If only . . .

You may have great plans for giving tomorrow. But tomorrow is a place of dreams. You may never see tomorrow. Your challenge is today.

Pile up a lot of tomorrows, and you wind up with a lot of empty yesterdays!

David served his generation, by the will of God. He could not serve the preceding generation, nor the next generation.

"Sufficient unto the day is the evil thereof" (Matthew 6:34).

Tomorrow will have its own problems. What are you doing about today? God has given you the present. Today. You'll never have it again.

God promised Abraham that through him and Isaac the entire world would be blessed. You are the seed of Abraham, and He wants to bless the entire world through you. That is the Obedience Dividend.

I ask you candidly, "Is the Great Commission of

Jesus Christ valid today?"

If it is, what are you doing to obey it? Can you think of a more effective way than to undergird the training of credentialed leaders in the "how" of evangelism so that they can return to evangelize their own people and train others to do the same?

God commanded Abraham. Abraham obeyed God. God blessed the world through Abraham's obedience.

What is God commanding you to do today? What will your response be? Obedience? Or disobedience? There is no middle ground. Only you know what God is commanding you to do. Only you can obey. No one else can make this decision for you.

With your obedience, the whole world will be blessed. And your epitaph will be an epitaph to the glory of God and truest blessings on multitudes for whom Christ died. Heaven's epitaph over your life will honor you as a believer who changed the world — for good. You will be one who claimed the Obedience Dividend.

10
CHRIST ABOVE ALL

"He must increase, but I must decrease."
And, *"He is above all."*
Who said so?

The man who Jesus said was the greatest born of woman.

What a testimony. And what a man!

He shouts with a loud voice, "Repent!"

The merchants up in Jerusalem closed their stores. The doctors quit their practices. The lawyers left their offices. The mechanics laid down their tools. The farmers down in Judea stopped plowing. And the women left their kitchens. All the country turned out to go down to the banks of the Jordan to hear this strange man, dressed in strange garb, deliver his strange message.

It follows that we will honor the Lord Jesus and enrich ourselves if we follow the example of John the Baptist.

He said, concerning Christ, *"He must increase, but I must decrease. He who comes from above is above all"* (John 3:30-31a).

Christ above all!

May God, the Holy Spirit, help me to show you what that implies — how that conviction molds our life.

Christ above all in His character

Examine the universality of His character, its completeness, and its moral perfection. When I lectured at the University of International Business and Economics in Beijing — some consider it the MIT of China — the graduate students asked me about Jesus. I told them. They sat with wide eyes and rapt attention as I explained the character of Jesus.

In 1968, on my first meeting with the President of Indonesia, Mr. Suharto looked me in the eye, and with his Mona Lisa smile and enigmatic conversational style, asked, "Are you here to proselytize Muslims to Christianity?"

In that tense moment, I silently called to the Lord for help.

Then I answered, "Excellency, I like your Pancasila." That's the Indonesian bill of rights. He registered surprise that I knew about the Pancasila and its five principles.

I said, "Is not the very first of the five principles freedom of religion?"

He assured me that it was.

Then I said, "I would like the high and holy honor of presenting Jesus Christ as a viable option for effective living."

He said, "That's fine." I had not offended him.

The generals, mostly Muslim, standing around him didn't seem offended either. Not only did my answer satisfy the President, he granted me unrestricted visa access to Indonesia. His closest associate told me I was the only nondiplomat to be given unrestricted access to the nation.

Believe me, it would have been a different story if I had told him I wanted to convert his people to a different religion.

The name Jesus found resonance in his mind.

Every man has some good points, but Jesus Christ had them all. He had them all in absolute perfection. He was the only impenitent man who ever lived. And He died that way. He prayed for others; He said, *"Father, forgive them"* (Luke 23:34), but He never prayed that way for Himself. He never prayed, "Father, forgive Me," because there was nothing in His life for which He needed to be forgiven.

Christ above all!

So I say, "Glance at the moral character of Jesus." There have been many noble characters in the world — glorious heroes, patriots, philanthropists, reformers, martyrs — men and women who justly deserve our respect.

Scientists tell us that carbon has some 60,000 known compounds. Combined with other elements, carbon creates countless familiar materials — wood, flesh, carbon dioxide, diamond. Yet carbon retains its identity without destroying the identity of a single element with which it bonds.

Carbon suggests the wondrous combining power of the ageless Christ, the desire of all nations, the heartthrob of history, the completion of the individual, the crown of the universe — who combines with red, yellow, black, and white, and in combining neither destroys the one with whom

He combines nor destroys Himself. He maintains His own perfection, while the one with whom He combines is more and more conformed to the Lord Jesus Christ.

The Apostle Paul reminds us that, in Christ,

> *. . . there is neither Greek nor Jew* (no racial boundary)*, neither uncircumcision nor circumcision* (no ritualistic boundary)*, Barbarian, Scythian* (no national boundary)*, nor bond nor free* (no social boundary)*, but Christ is all and in all* (Colossians 3:11).

He loves the red man, God's image in cedar. He loves the yellow man, God's image in boxwood. He loves the brown man, God's image in mahogany. He loves the black man, God's image in ebony. And He even loves the white man, God's image in poplar.

How do you account for the personality of Jesus? Recall the age in which He lived — an age of Jewish traditionalism, conceit, bigotry; an age of Caesarean imperialism, selfishness, brutality, atheism. Yet, in spite of all of this, Jesus of Nazareth is earth's solitary ideal, time's transcendent miracle. Instead of Christ's character having been the product of His age, His character was an absolute anachronism.

How happens it that Jerusalem with her temple, Egypt with her Heliopolis, Athens with her Academy, Rome with her Forum, France with her Sorbonne, Germany with her Heidelberg, England with her Oxford, America with her Harvard — how happens it that these, and all such as these, have never produced a peer, at best only dim hints, of the Nazarene?

How would you account for the personality of Jesus?

Our wonder grows when we reflect that:

- He wrote no book, no poem, no drama, no philosophy
- He invented no tool or instrument
- He fashioned no law for enactment
- He discovered no medicine or remedy
- He outlined no philosophy of mind or body
- He contributed nothing to geology or astronomy

Rather, he stood at the end of His brief earthly career, doomed and deserted, solitary and silent, utterly helpless, facing a shameless trial and a pitiless execution.

The ages have come and gone. Yet the carpenter's son has lifted the gates of empires off their hinges, turned the streams of the centuries out of their channels, leavened all literature, and made laws just, governments humane, manners gentle, even cold marble warm. He has refined art for new and divine themes, inspired those "frozen prayers" we call cathedrals, led scientists to dedicate their books and discoveries to Him.

He so glorified an instrument of torture that the very queen among beautiful women seeks to enhance her loveliness by hanging His cross about her neck, while new inventions and institutions seem but letters in His storied speech.

Today, no one's birthday but His is celebrated in all nations.

Christ above all in His works

Jesus said, *"The works that I do, bear witness of me that the Father sent me"* (John 5:36).

He takes the rich and shows them how really poor and naked they are. He takes the self-sufficient and shows them how really dependent they are. He takes the moral man and the moral woman, strips them of worthless rags of self-righteousness, and redeems them one and all to a new and powerful life.

To sum up the works of our Lord: He continues to reorganize human chaos, reverse human instincts, revolutionize human tendencies, coordinate human faculties, transfigure human sensibilities, marshal human powers, disclose human potentialities, give human character a gilded celestial edge.

The Babe of Bethlehem is the contemporary of all times; the Man of Calvary is the inhabitant of all lands.

More than a hundred years ago, Presbyterian missionaries from Ohio sailed to the far away city of Damascus, the world's oldest, continuously inhabited city. No serenading orchestra greeted them on arrival. No red carpet had been rolled out for their access to the open arms of waiting royalty.

No hotels existed for their shelter. No restaurants, as we know them today, had been established for their meals while waiting to get settled.

They committed their total time and energies there for a full four years. They believed the words they sang: "Wherever He leads I'll go."

During those four years, they had to forego attendance at family members' graduations in the States. They could not return for the burial of their loved ones, or the weddings of their own flesh and blood. On average, one out of every four of them died and was buried under the Syrian skies.

In the course of time, these dear soldiers of the Cross won to faith in Christ a young Syrian man. He became a colporteur who distributed Bibles and religious literature.

He visited a businessman who had been felled by a stroke — one of the more astute and unscrupulous businessmen in the city. The young colporteur offered the caustic businessman a Bible. The businessman replied harshly. He was partially paralyzed. He couldn't get off his mat. The timid colporteur placed the Bible as close to him as he dared. He said, "I'll come back in a year. If you decide to keep it, you can pay me. Otherwise, I will take it back."

After a few weeks of intolerable boredom, the businessman looked at that Bible. Then he picked it up and began to read.

The Holy Spirit graciously, through the reading of Scripture, brought him to Christ.

He became a powerful witness for the Lord. He

founded a Presbyterian seminary. He won to faith in Christ his ten-year-old nephew. Five years later, the nephew, along with two brothers, fled from under the oppression of the Ottoman Empire's tyrannical leaders.

After he arrived in America, this same young Syrian entered the Moody Bible Institute for study. There he met a lady of English ancestry whom he married.

Out of that union came four boys, whose characters were molded by the godly influence of their home.

The second son, in 1971, received the L.A. Hyland Award for scientific achievement. The citation read at the presentation of the award credited the young scientist's inventions with saving untold thousands of lives and saving the government billions of dollars in military equipment.

Talk about good stewardship! The few thousand dollars spent on those Presbyterian missionaries to Syria, America — yes, and the world — have received back in thousands of lives and multimillions of dollars.

The youngest son in 1971 was given the Boy Scouts' highest honor, the Silver Buffalo Award — presented in the Atlanta Civic Center. The citation that went with that award accoladed the recipient as having had enormous influence in quieting the unrest in the exploding university campuses across America.

The oldest son writes the account you are now reading.

Matchless influence of Jesus!

The matchless works of Jesus Christ, still visible in His people today.

Christ above all in His command

I have bent every effort in prayer, preparation, and presentation to impress you with Jesus — unique, august, supreme.

My passion centers on leading you to the blood-earnest conclusion that believers ignore His command at their peril.

The awareness of His sovereign authority strips away every excuse — plausible or blatant — of disobedience at this point.

> *And Jesus came and spake unto them, saying,*
> *All authority is given unto me in heaven*
> *and in earth. Go ye, therefore, and teach*
> *all nations, baptizing them in the name of*
> *the Father, and of the Son, and of the Holy*
> *Ghost: Teaching them to observe all things*
> *whatsoever I have commanded you: and lo, I*
> *am with you always, even unto the end of the*
> *world. Amen* (Matthew 28:18-20 KJV).

To ignore this constitutes disobedience of the Great Commission and insubordination to our Commander in Chief, the Great Commissioner! Furthermore, it creates universal genocide! Think about that. Millions dying in their sins and spending eternity in hell.

Our response reveals our focus. It proves or disproves what we say. Do we live out our testimony "He must increase and I must decrease"? Or does our disobedience scream out our self-centered belief that "I must increase and He must decrease" — that I, not Christ, am "above all"?

The most persistent command of Jesus to His followers? Take the Gospel to the whole world.

Unfortunately, we have trifled with these Divine orders. Our response could be termed, in some instances, a mockery. Churches in the United States direct less than 2 percent of their total income to non-West, nonwhite, overseas evangelism.

Had we sent the Gospel to countries of the Arabic-speaking world when they were open, there may never have been the attacks on 11 September 2001. I don't mean the terrorists would all have come to Christ.

I do mean it would have framed the free world in such a way they would have carried different images in their hearts.

We didn't take that opportunity. As a result, many in the Arabic-speaking world resent the free world's living standard, educational opportunities, and power of choice. Their inability to get education, wealth, and unrestricted movement has made them bitter and suicidal, as well as homicidal.

I cannot understand the self-delusion that makes us think we are mission-minded when we had within our power the opportunity to be God's instruments of temporal and eternal change for His glory, the world's blessing, and our benefit.

Dr. John R. Mott — my great hero of the 20th century, whom I met when I was a teenage boy — said in 1906, after the Russo-Japanese War, "Give me 1,000 missionaries for Japan, or in 50 years we'll be sending 100,000 of our boys with guns and bayonets."

We didn't give him 1,000. We gave him six. That's all. And he was wrong, of course. It wasn't 50 years; it was 36 years. It wasn't 100,000 of our boys; it was over a million of our boys — and girls. It wasn't guns and bayonets; it was the atomic bomb.

Christ above all!

And what of those who possess the power to be God's instruments — and yet give it away to others who have no passion for the Gospel?

There are numerous foundations established by Bible-believing grantors who left the distribution of billions of dollars to men and women who never did share their priority, in some cases to trustees who look upon Jesus as a mere man.

I will give you one example: the Kresge Foundation. I knew Stanley Kresge well, and his wife Dorothy. They liked my book *How to Win Over Worry*. Mrs. Dorothy Kresge wrote me to tell me that, during their devotional time each morning, they were reading a chapter out of that book. It did not replace their reading of Scripture, of course.

So committed to her firm beliefs in the Word of God was she that when the stores founded by that great family opened on Sunday, she unloaded all of her stock. Her advisors warned her that unloading such a vast amount of stock would depress the market and decimate the price.

No matter. She was not going to compromise her convictions.

I have learned that the Kresge Foundation now funds the NPR — National Public Radio — which must be one of the most staunchly secular entities in the United States today.

What results could have been realized if those millions had been used to spread the Gospel of our Lord's redeeming love?

Thank God there are some who take it seriously.

P. K. D. Lee was on a fast track to go to the top of the world's largest employer — soon to have been made number-one of one of their nine zones. Why would he leave and spend the past 18 years, with a brutalizing travel schedule to all nations of the world, in his effort to do his part in bringing the Gospel to the ends of the earth?

It's Christ above all.

Why would our personnel around the world put in the hours they put in, and sacrificially give over and above their church tithe in order to carry out our Lord's sovereign command? And not only do they give themselves, but they have enlisted their families to give as well.

What it means to obey Christ's command can be summarized in four questions.

1. Is Christ above all in your time?

Scriptures teach us that time is short — and that we must redeem the time: *"Redeeming the time for the days are evil"* (Ephesians 5:16). Jesus said, *"I must do the works of him that sent me while it is yet day; the night cometh when no man can work"* (John 9:4).

Haggai Institute's annual meeting presents our only opportunity to disclose the realities of this ministry in nations hostile to the Gospel. To present this ministry by radio, television, or the print medium would jeopardize the lives of many of our people.

Enemies of the Cross of Christ know exactly what we do. They write about us in their national magazines.

That is why I have asked my good friend and famous broadcaster Paul Harvey not to use my name on any of his broadcasts. That is why I declined the gracious invitation of Dr. James Dobson to be his guest on his *Focus on the Family* radio program. That is why we go to such extremes to stay out of the public eye.

The situation continues to be explosive. So far five Haggai Institute alumni have been martyred. We have 12,000 graduates working in the Islamic world, including Afghanistan and Iraq.

A few years ago, one of my dearest friends, a trustee of this ministry, told me that he was just too busy — he could not come to the annual meeting.

He is a disciplined world leader. He listens to reason and faces facts.

I told him his attendance would take only 30 hours of his time. He has written brilliantly on time control. I consider him one of the most skilled in planning his time budget.

I repeated his own written emphasis that each person has 168 hours a week. That's 8,736 hours a year.

I said, "In Jesus' name, I am asking you to take just 3/10ths of 1 percent of your time for this year to come to this annual meeting. Your presence makes an impact. And you need to know what's taking place in the dangerous places of the world."

The good sport that he is, and the honest man that he is, he chuckled and said, "I'll be there."

Study the life of the Apostle Paul in the first century, or of Francis Xavier in the sixteenth century.

In ten years, Xavier learned and preached the Gospel in 20 different languages as he moved from Europe all the way to the Orient. He often put in a 20-hour day. He administers the most stinging rebuke to apathy I know.

There is no Pentecost without plenty-cost.

When we fail to marshal our hours to carry out His command, we are saying, in effect, "I must increase, He must decrease."

2. Is Christ above all in your priorities?

What is important to us gets our attention.

The Apostle Paul said to Timothy: *"I exhort therefore, that, first of all, supplications, prayers, intercessions, and giving of thanks be made for all men; for kings, and for all that are in authority; that we may lead a quiet and peaceable life in all godliness and honesty"* (1 Timothy 2:1-2).

In reality, how many of us could follow that instruction? How many of us know who leads another country until his name is plastered all over the headlines of our newspapers?

3. Is Christ above all in your relationships?

When I entered the field of evangelism, I recruited a young man to handle the youth ministry. He was handsome, quick-witted, affable, a veritable magnet to young people. I thought he was totally committed to Christ.

He kept hesitating to move to Atlanta from Texas.

When I pressed him for the reason, he said they were expecting a baby. I congratulated him and asked what that had to do with his move.

He said they wanted the same doctor who delivered him and his wife to deliver the baby.

Hardly believing what he was saying, I asked, "Where does the Lord's leadership enter into your thinking?" He would not budge.

His selection of a doctor overrode his commitment to the Lord's work.

With broken heart I had to accept his resignation.

He was not willing to put Christ first in his relationships. It was not *"Christ above all."* It was, "I must increase, He must decrease."

In my first pastorate in 1944, a devoted young couple of our church broke the great news that after seven years of marriage she was finally expecting a child. We were all rejoicing.

The baby's arrival tragically altered their lifestyle. No longer was Christ above all; now it was baby above all. They stopped attending church. Whatever the child wanted, the child got.

At age seven, the child died inexplicably. They brokenheartedly recognized their sin, repented of it, came back to the Lord and served Him faithfully until the Lord took them Home a few years ago.

No one can carry out the explicit command of our Lord when they elevate relationships to lordship. That's tantamount to saying, "I must increase, He must decrease."

4. Is Christ above all in your financial planning?

Many years ago I was told that more than $100 million goes intestate in Los Angeles County each month! (It's likely higher than that today.) Suppose that 5 percent of those people were believers who took seriously the word and work of the Lord. That would represent $5 million of that $100 million. They didn't take time to plan and make out their wills. Mindlessly they assigned the distribution of their estate to the government.

Ten percent (10%) of that 5 million is $500,000 every month — in other words, $6 million lost every year to the cause of Christ in just one county of one state of the 50 states in this one nation.

Meaning? "I must increase. He must decrease." Not "Christ above all."

A visiting minister heard me, a 14-year-old boy, make an excuse to my dad. He said, "Young man, never forget that an excuse is the skin of a reason stuffed with a lie."

Christ above all in financial planning? Here is one excuse: I've turned over the distribution of charitable funds to the children.

I can't help asking, "Were you responsible for the accumulation of any of the funds?" They respond with a certain justifiable pride over the hard work that created the wealth.

I say, "How can you delegate to others who may not have your value system, even if they are family members? How can you shirk your responsibility? To which of your family members have you delegated your prayer time? To which of your family members have you delegated your Bible study time? To which of your family members have you delegated your church attendance? And to which of your family members have you delegated your witnessing responsibilities?"

Another excuse: You know, I'm retired.

A retired couple very close to my wife, Christine, and me has refused to retire from their stewardship opportunities. They spend more time now planning strategy for maximum giving than they did 30 years ago in their 50s.

Each year they give to each of their children.

They ask each child to give a specific percentage to Haggai Institute. One year one child kept the amount, so the next year they told him, "We're adding to our gifts to Haggai Institute this year what you kept last year and deducting it from this year's gift to you."

I have a cherished friend in Abu Dhabi. He trades currencies on the Forex, which is the world's largest market. Every day between $2 trillion and $3 trillion are traded.

He attended our Special Leadership Seminar in Maui. At dinner one evening, I said, "Tell me about your plans for the next 20 years."

He told me he was 48 years old and planned to retire at 50. I said, "Why?" He told me that's the custom in his part of the world. I asked him why he would not continue trading on his own and give the profits to the Lord's work. The light turned on. I can never forget his smile.

Another excuse: I make my money where I live, so I give my money to my community.

I remind them it's not their money. It's God's money. As Moses said in Deuteronomy, *"It is God who gives you the power to get wealth"* (Deuteronomy 8:18).

But the question is: "Who is above all? Is Christ above all, or not?"

Another excuse: My children complain that I am giving away their inheritance.

That I don't even understand. Have they not brought up their children in the nurture and admonition of the Lord — in the truth of Scripture? The question will not be silenced, "Is Christ above all, or are your children above all?"

Of course you want to provide for them, give them a good education, and probably help on a first home. I often ask close friends, "Where would you be today if your father had done for you what you are doing for your children?" Think about it. I repeat — "Is it Christ above all, or your children above all?"

Another excuse: I'm expected to give to this civic event or social project.

That's fine. But Jesus Christ did not say, "Give all your money to hometown social projects." He did say, *"Go into all the world and preach the Gospel."* Is it Christ above all, or social prestige above all?

By the grace of God, Haggai Institute alumni are in every Islamic area of the world, throughout China, and in every state in India. Each graduate commits to train 100 others within 24 months of returning home. Some have trained several hundred.

A retired general in Brazil has trained over 4,000. He gave me a large binder with their names, ages, vocations, and church affiliations.

The Haggai Institute supporters on a 2003 vision journey met Dr. S. J. Sutjiono, who has trained more than 20,000.

Our trustees underwrite all administrative and fundraising costs. That means every dollar you give goes directly to training. Every dollar does the work of a hundred dollars because of the multiplying principle: each graduate training 100 others.

I frequently speak of Cecil Day. A quarter century after his death, his name is known and respected across the world. Why? Because of the Days Inn hotel chain? No — because he put Christ above all in his finances. And thanks to his sacrificial giving we were able to acquire the Day Center in Singapore and literally put this ministry on the map.

Ask yourself, "What does Christ want me to do? He has given me the command — the unspeakable opportunity. How will I respond?"

I started by telling you of John the Baptist. This man of outstanding ability, concerning whom our Lord said was the greatest born of women, turned his back on the life of ease, and put himself on the stretch for God. He preached repentance for his six months' ministry prior to his execution by Herod. His entire life shouted out the truth of his life motto: *He must increase, I must decrease. He is above all. Christ above all.*

George Whitefield, whom God used to start The Great Awakening in the 18th Century in the Colonies, was preaching in an open field.

Benjamin Franklin came to hear him. Benjamin Franklin estimated the crowd at 21,000. Then he started listening to George Whitefield.

He decided he would give him a dollar for the orphanage for which Whitefield was raising money. He kept listening and decided to raise it to five dollars. He said at the end of the message he gave everything he had in his pocket — over a hundred dollars.

He told his friend about that, and his friend said, "Oh, you were just moved by his oratory." Franklin replied, "It was not his oratory, but the cause."

Forget my message, but remember the cause: Obedience to the Great Commission, the winning of the world to Christ. You and I must decrease. He must increase.

Christ above all!

INDEX

John Edmund Haggai
Founder and Chairman
Haggai Institute

John Edmund Haggai has been called a visionary, a Christian world statesman, an evangelist, and a master of the pulpit, all of which is true of this dynamic man of God.

Never content to follow the crowd, Dr. Haggai initiated a unique and forward-thinking mission plan in obedience to the Great Commission. A visit to Asia in the early 1960s convinced Haggai that changes in global geopolitics, brought about by the end of colonialism, required a new strategy for world evangelism. In 1969, after years of research, prayer, and development, he presided over the first advanced leadership seminar, designed to empower and mobilize nationals to reach their own people for Christ.

Today, more than 65,500 Christian clergy and lay leaders have been trained. They currently work in 178 nations. The numbers multiply significantly as the graduates pass on their training to an average of 100 others.

After more than sixty years in public service, this man shows no signs of slowing down in his work for the Kingdom. He continues to lead the ministry, write his memoirs, and speak in churches, universities, seminaries, and business groups throughout the world.

Dr. Haggai, alumnus of Moody Bible Institute (where he was named Alumnus of the Year) and Furman University, has garnered many awards and earned honorary doctorates from both sides of the Pacific.

He has authored more than a dozen books, including *How to Win Over Worry, My Son Johnny, Lead On!*, and *The Leading Edge.*

John Edmund Haggai was born in Louisville, Kentucky, son of a Syrian immigrant and a New Englander whose English ancestors settled in America during the 1600s. He and wife Christine live in Atlanta, Georgia; however, their influence touches millions around the globe.

Haggai Institute

PO Box 13

Atlanta

Georgia 30370-2801

U.S.A.

Telephone: 1-770-449-8869

Toll free in U.S.: 1-800-642-4424

Website: www.haggai-institute.com

HAGGAI INSTITUTE
A Better Tool for the Great Commission

WHAT WE DO
Haggai Institute gains powerful access for the Gospel in a world increasingly resistant to Western missionaries.

HOW WE DO IT
We seek out influential Christians in developing nations. We give them life-changing training at one of our world-class training centers in Singapore or Maui. Then we send them home with advanced leadership skills and a commitment to train 100 other Christian leaders. We call this THE EXPO FACTOR.

WHY WE'RE HERE
The age in which conventional missionary work flourished is gone forever. Massive population growth and fragmented geopolitics are today's realities, forcing a new strategy for missions. In the twenty-first century, those best equipped to change the world for Christ are those who already occupy leadership positions in their own nations, companies, and communities.

WHERE WE OPERATE
We have trained multiple tens of thousands of Christian leaders, from nations representing almost the entire population of the non-Western world. Through these leaders we impact every kind of frontline Christian ministry. A large percentage of our graduates work in regions, like the Middle East, that are highly resistant to Christian faith.

WHO WE ARE
Haggai Institute brings together exceptional Christian leaders — men and women, lay and ordained — from a wealth of Christian traditions. Our donor base is international. Thanks to THE EXPO FACTOR, all receive a huge return on their investment in the Great Commission.

Notes

Notes

Notes

Notes

Notes

Notes

Notes

Notes

Notes

Notes

Notes

Notes

Notes

Notes

Notes

Notes

Notes

Notes

Notes

Notes

Notes

Notes

Notes

Notes

Notes

Notes

Notes

Notes

Notes

Notes

Notes

Notes